SINK
OR
SWIM

**Milo Sindell
and Thuy Sindell, Ph.D.**

Adams Media
Avon, Massachusetts

Published by Adams Media, an F+W Publications Company
57 Littlefield Street
Avon, MA 02322
www.adamsmedia.com

ISBN: 1-59337-540-9

Printed in the United States of America.

J   I   H   G   F   E   D   C   B   A

Library of Congress Cataloging-in-Publication Data
Sindell, Milo.
sink or swim: new job. new boss. 12 weeks to get it right. / Milo Sindell
and Thuy Sindell.
p.   cm.
Includes index.
ISBN 1-59337-540-9
1. Success in business. 2. Work. 3. Self-presentation. 4. Career development.
I. Sindell, Thuy. II. Title.
HF5386.S55 2006
650.1—dc22
2005026069

This publication is designed to provide accurate and authoritative information with regard
to the subject matter covered. It is sold with the understanding that the publisher is not
engaged in rendering legal, accounting, or other professional advice. If legal advice or
other expert assistance is required, the services of a competent professional person should
be sought.

—From a *Declaration of Principles* jointly adopted by a
Committee of the American Bar Association and
a Committee of Publishers and Associations

Many of the designations used by manufacturers and sellers to distinguish their product are
claimed as trademarks. Where those designations appear in this book and Adams Media was
aware of a trademark claim, the designations have been printed with initial capital letters.

This book is available at quantity discounts for bulk purchases.
For information, please call 1-800-872-5627.

CONTENTS

ACKNOWLEDGMENTS

We would like to acknowledge all sets of parents who inspired us to always be and do our best. In particular, we want to thank Gerald Sindell for his input and support of the book from start to finish. Thank you for helping us find our voice.

Thank you to our book agent, Michael Snell, and acquisition editor, Jill Alexander, for your enthusiasm regarding the power, impact, and potential of *Sink or Swim.*

We want to thank Sue Bethanis, Anthony Perry, and Jeff Sanders for your high-level and detailed review of the book. Your input was tremendously valuable to the end product. Thank you for making the time in your crazy schedules to make this a priority.

Finally, we want to acknowledge the professional influences in our life including Marshall Goldsmith, Beverly Kaye, Sal Falletta, and Sue Bethanis. Thank you for your generosity and guidance.

USER INSTRUCTIONS

Congratulations! You worked hard to find the right company, did all the right things to make your resume rise to the top of the pile, and aced the interviews. Now you've got the job. They chose you.

You are embarking on an adventure that requires swimming in uncharted waters. Your destination is clear: success in your new job! However, getting to your destination will require that you stay on course, make savvy decisions, and stay afloat.

In your hands is your new-employee life vest: a week-by-week guide to achieving great things during the first twelve weeks on the job. Whether you are starting your job next week or have already begun, today is the day you jump in and start swimming.

Maximum success in your new job requires that you be your own champion. What does being your own champion mean? You have the power to control the choices you make. Specifically, that you:

1. Always look for opportunities in every situation.
2. Know your strengths and where you contribute value.
3. Know when and how to ask for help.

This book provides you with the *5 Sink or Swim skills* you need to master in order to be your own champion and succeed!

Why Does It Matter?

Over the past forty years, the implied social agreement between employers and employees has changed. Employers, under the old contract, acted as parental figures and provided employees with a lifetime of structure and support in exchange for hard work and loyalty.

Today, the concept of lifetime employment is unimaginable and probably undesirable. The fact is that over time most people get bored and benefit from a change. Even worse, if you are reporting to a boss who does not treat you particularly well, years of employment in the same situation can be profoundly demoralizing.

What's important for you to understand is that you own your career. You are responsible for setting professional goals, identifying and developing the right skills, and building your resume. Every time you develop new skills, you become even more valuable in the job market.

Companies also understand that the contract has changed: Employees aren't married to the company anymore. To retain their employees, companies must offer a range of benefits. Smart companies understand that it not only takes a competitive salary to attract and retain good employees, but it also takes programs that support the employees' needs and interests.

Smart companies, however, also know that all of these benefits are not enough to keep the best employees from going to the competition. Therefore, they strive to provide opportunities for employees to learn new skills or change jobs within the company in order to keep people engaged and motivated.

However smart companies may be, you as an employee must also be smart and make the most out of your job. You have two responsibilities.

1. A responsibility to your company to do what you were hired to do.
2. A responsibility to yourself to develop your skills, create and identify opportunities, and manage your career.

Your company should be clear about what it expects of you; however, you must also take charge and be clear about your expectations of your employer. What do you want in exchange for contributing your skills, abilities, and expertise? Besides your salary and health insurance benefits, what else do you want? What about learning opportunities so you can have more skills and be more marketable? What about career advancement? What about a positive work environment? You won't get what you want if you don't know what you want. When you have both sets of expectations clearly defined (i.e., for your company and yourself), you will be able to provide the maximum value to your company and in return have your own needs met. *Sink or Swim* will give you the skills and tools to strengthen your relationship with your employer and be your own champion.

How to Use This Book

We know what it is like to start a new job. It is both exciting and nerve-racking. Most of all, it is an opportunity. In your hands is a resource that we would have loved to have had as new employees. It is a compilation of our knowledge, experience, and best practices assembled into a user-friendly format.

Read the *5 Sink or Swim skills* areas in this section before you start your job. Like anything else, it is important to understand what you need to do and why before you actually go do it. Each chapter will provide you with weekly detailed information about how to apply the *5 Sink or Swim skills* explained in this introductory section. During your first twelve weeks at work, use the corresponding week as your guide to focus and develop the right skills at the right time, plan your activities, and build momentum toward success.

If you are getting ready to interview for a job, read this section. It will give you a head start. You'll take away some ideas about questions to ask about the company as well as questions about the job for which you are interviewing.

If you have already started your job, it's not too late. It's time to jump in now! Read this entire introduction before your next day at work and make sure you do everything mentioned in each of the weeks until you catch up to your current week.

Your mission is to get up to speed as quickly as possible in your first twelve weeks on the job. Why twelve weeks? In most companies, there is a period of approximately ninety days in which you and the company decide if this new arrangement will work out. That's why first impressions matter. Ninety days is not a long time. Therefore, it is critical that you swim with the current and keep your head above water. Remember, people are watching and paying attention to you; use it positively to your advantage.

This book helps you figure out what you need to do as you go through each workday and -week: set goals, establish milestones, develop contacts, and build relationships. Each week is different and builds on the work you did in the previous week. Throughout the first twelve weeks you will gather information, think about what you are learning, apply it, and continuously fine-tune your *Sink or Swim* skills.

Learning is a dynamic and ongoing process. What does that mean? Dynamic means learning is in motion—you read something in the book, try it out in real life, and then go back to the book and read even more carefully and try it again. What does ongoing mean? A healthy person never stops learning.

You may find that these *5 Sink or Swim skills* make sense and are obvious and foundational. You're right! You might also say to yourself "I can do this already." Maybe you can. Terrific! We are willing to bet that there is opportunity to integrate and apply these skills even better than you can now. We challenge you to take these *Sink or Swim* skills one step further and make a positive difference in your new job. There are a lot of exciting opportunities that come with starting a new job. Here is the guide to help you succeed.

The *5 Sink or Swim Skills*

The goal of this book is to ensure that you make the most of this new opportunity by applying the right *Sink or Swim* skills at the right time. Here's what you will learn.

 GOALS Get clear on your role, responsibilities, projects, and where you want to be in your new company and career. Set goals to get you where you want to be.

 TIME Learn the most important elements of effective time management and fine-tune how to apply them for maximum results. Be productive and focused.

 KNOWLEDGE Get the right knowledge to do your job, develop your network of resources, identify ways to develop your own skills, and share what you know with others. Have the right information when you need it and demonstrate your value to others.

TEAM Learn what it means to be a team player and how to be one even if you are not a part of a team. Work well with others and build a lasting network of partnerships.

IMAGE You will focus on the skills and subtle intricacies of identifying and crafting the right professional image. Clearly communicate who you are and what you stand for.

To make the *5 Sink or Swim skills* easy to recognize while you're reading, each skill is represented by a symbol (as in the preceding list). The symbols are placed throughout the book to help show where you are along your path to success.

All of the *5 Sink or Swim skills* are interrelated. As you read, take notes. If no pen is available, dog-ear the page as you read. This book is meant to be used. The following section explains the *Sink or Swim* skills, why they are important, and how they pertain to your job. As you read the following section of this chapter, don't get bogged down and worry about mastering the *Sink or Swim* skills. The weekly chapters will take you step-by-step through each of the skills and guide you on how to apply the skills while on the job.

These *5 Sink or Swim skills* may seem obvious to you, but knowing it is not the same thing as doing it. This is your opportunity to further develop your *Sink or Swim* skills and put them into practice. In fact, many managers and executives pay tens of thousands of dollars in consulting fees for help in learning to apply these same skills. It is lucky for you; you're going to save a lot of money and help yourself get off to a great start in your new position.

Goals

Your new job holds many promising opportunities. To make the most of them, you must first define what you want. Most of us often talk about what we want, but few of us actually achieve our dreams. The reason this happens is because we don't set effective goals.

Turning your desires into goals requires a different level of commitment. When you have clearly defined goals, you no longer sit back and wait for things to happen. Rather, you are an active participant and make things happen. Clearly defined goals mean that every little thing you do is part of something bigger toward which you are building. It gives each task meaning and a bigger context. This section shows you how to set and achieve your goals.

At the end of the twelve weeks, you will have set six-month and one-year goals that have personal significance and are achievable. Most of us have a tendency to set goals that are not realistic, not goals that we are truly committed to . . . like starving yourself to lose ten pounds in one week to fit into that black pair of pants you bought on sale that was one size too small.

Effective goals require that you do the following:

1. Create achievable goals.
2. Commit to your goals.
3. Determine what success looks like.
4. Design the plan to get you to your goal.

Create Achievable Goals

The likelihood of accomplishing your goals is increased when you stick to a few basics.

▶ Set goals that are realistic and provide a challenge.
▶ Set goals that do not contradict any of your other goals.
▶ Set goals that are in your control.
▶ Set goals that are positive and reflect what you really want.

When it comes to your goals, size does matter. You have to be realistic. If you set a goal to end world hunger, it will feel like you are staring down a tidal wave. It's a wonderful aspiration, and it is not realistic. That doesn't mean that you should throw away your goal. Break your big goal down to more manageable chunks. When you do that, you may find that there are four smaller goals that lead to your bigger goal.

Let's say you really want to take on world hunger . . . good for you! Start with a smaller-size goal such as ending hunger in your local community. Then proceed to the state level and so on. When you define the components that make up your goals, you break even the largest and wildest ambition into manageable chunks. It is important to challenge yourself. What's the point of setting a mediocre goal that only makes you relatively happy and merely satisfied versus setting a goal that is going to push you to try harder and give it your best?

Your goals also cannot contradict each other. Let's say your goal is to save enough money for a down payment for your first home within the next year and you simultaneously want to try all the finest restaurants in your town. These two goals can be tough to reach since they contradict each other. If your goal is to save money, the finest restaurants will have to wait.

Set goals in a manner that gives you ownership and pushes you to try your best. Sometimes we establish goals that require or depend upon things we cannot control. You can't push yourself to try your best when you don't even have control over the outcome. There will be none of that here! Let's say you want your boss to respect you. This is a common desire; most people want their boss's respect. By setting the goal that "I want my boss to respect me," you give control to your boss. The outcome would not be in your control nor would it require you to take ownership of what you need to do in order to succeed.

A goal that would provide a similar outcome and be in your control is "I will build a positive relationship with my boss by providing regular updates and having a clear understanding of her expectations of me so that she will respect me." Note the difference. In the description of the second goal, you have identified the steps that you control and upon which you can act.

Finally, state your objectives and the behavior required in a positive way. For example, the goal "I will not miss my deadlines" emphasizes your current negative behavior of missing deadlines. When you state this goal in the positive, "I will hit my deadlines," you focus on the future and what you need to do to make this happen. Your words shape a positive direction for your efforts. Your attention is now focused on the good things that you will do differently.

Commit to Your Goals

Now that you know what you want, it is important to understand why you want it. Is it enough that you want to lose weight, or are you truly committed to it? Most of us set goals to which we are not really committed. Without commitment, your goals will not be achieved. When you are clear on why you want a particular goal, the goal has a deeper, more personal meaning. You increase the likelihood that you will keep on track, even during those times when you may feel overwhelmed or distracted.

Finally, write your goals down. It's amazing how people don't do that and then very quickly forget what they wanted to achieve. When you write down your goal, it is your first step toward making it a reality. Something very powerful occurs when you transfer an idea into a physical form. You are making a declaration. Use it everyday as a visual reminder. You'd be amazed how much more positive goal setting can be when you see what you want to accomplish in writing.

Determine What Success Looks Like

If you ask someone who has achieved their goals how they did it, you will usually find that they had a way to score their progress. That means they always knew if they were getting closer to their goals and also were clear on when they achieved their goals. They knew what success looked like.

Define what success looks like for your goals.

- ▶ *What will be different?*—What will be different today versus where you were yesterday?
- ▶ *What will you see?*—What will the finished product look like? Will people be more interested to talk with you? Will you get more invitations to meetings? An award? Recognition from your team?
- ▶ *What will you hear?*—How will you talk about your achievement with others? What will people say when you achieve your goal? Will they have had a positive experience working with you?
- ▶ *How will you feel?*—Relieved? Delighted? Excited? Will it have been a positive experience? Will you have worked hard?

Once you are clear what your goal looks like, it's easier to create an action plan. You know exactly in which direction you are moving.

Design the Plan to Get You to Your Goal

After you have identified your goals, the next step is to design a plan that will take you to where you have set your sights. An effective plan will be your map. It will identify milestones, tasks, time, and resources to reach your goals.

When you develop your plan, focus on the following key elements:

- ▶ *Milestones*—Identify the major points of your project that must be completed. For example, an early milestone may be that you need to enlist the support of key contributors to your project.
- ▶ *Tasks*—Identify the more minute tasks that make up your milestones. For example, in order to enlist support, you will need to call each person and set a meeting time and date.
- ▶ *Time*—Give yourself a realistic time frame for completion of each of your milestones and tasks. For example, for your milestone, you may give yourself one month's time to make sure everyone is on board. The task of calling each person to set a time to meet can be done within one week.
- ▶ *Resources*—Determine the things you need to reach your goal. For example, besides meeting with key contributors to the project, what other information do you need? What about a budget or additional skills that will be required to complete the project?

Your plan should reflect the simplicity or complexity of your goals. Short-term or smaller goals may only require a task list. Larger goals may require a plan that outlines milestones, tasks, time frames, your existing skills, skills that require development, and resources required for reaching a goal. Use the day-by-day calendar at the end of each weekly chapter or your own calendar to map out when you want to complete a goal and when you need to accomplish specific milestones and tasks.

 Time

Time management . . . yuck! How many times have you said that to yourself? Time management seems to be one of those things that everybody needs to do, but few are actually good at it. The reality is that good time management is a necessity in the business world. Now, don't run and hide from it just yet. Breathe in. Breathe out. Relax! It'll be fine. *Sink or Swim* will help you learn—painlessly—how to be a great time manager one easy step at a time. You'll learn how to focus on the planning process, how to be realistic in allotting the appropriate amount of time to each task, and how to stick to your schedule.

Time management is not just about meeting deadlines and showing up for work on time. Effective time-management skills powerfully communicate to others that you are a winner—focused, reliable, consistent, and professional.

Planning

Good planning is the secret to successfully managing your time. Planning means you regularly think ahead to choose exactly what you want to accomplish and allocate the appropriate amount of time amid all the distractions and interruptions of the workday. To begin, take two to five minutes at the beginning of every week to set the stage. Then every day, take two to five minutes to create and/or review your task list. It does not take much time to create and update your task list. It takes discipline. The reward? Your priorities will snap into focus, and you will always know where you are in your day and what you can realistically accomplish.

Be aware that managing your time does not mean that you can always control your time. The unexpected will happen, and you must allow room for surprises. To better cope with unpredictability, you can control the way your day starts. Start your day with a morning routine that gives you time to seize the day. The magic of the right morning routine is that you start your day off ready and prepared for whatever comes your way. You can give yourself maximum predictability in a world of chaos.

Time Allocation

Most task lists and planning fall apart because people don't give themselves enough time to get the job completed. Can you think of a time when you thought you'd get something done in two hours and found it really took four? As you look back, can you see anything in particular that caused you to run overtime? Life and work are full of distractions. Maybe someone popped in for a quick chat; maybe you had a meeting that ran over. There are always the usual delays: heavy traffic, urgent e-mails, computer crashes, and unexpected phone calls.

As interruptions surface, you are often expected to respond as soon as possible. That's why you will need to create a time buffer if you're going to stick to your daily plan. This means giving yourself enough leeway to complete tasks—despite the inevitable distractions and interruptions. Be realistic and accurate when you schedule events, and remember to take the interruptions into account. In this way, you set yourself up for success.

Keep on Track with Your Schedule

Imagine that you have planned realistically and given yourself enough time to complete your projects. Great! Now, here is the last piece of the puzzle: keeping track of your schedule. Have you ever had the experience of getting into what seemed like a brief conversation with someone and it was so interesting that you simply lost track of time? Now imagine that happening as you're dashing from one meeting to another. It is absolutely guaranteed that people are going to stop you in the hallway and absolutely guaranteed that people will poke their heads into your cubicle or office for a quick question. Some of these interruptions are going to be important, and some are going to interfere with your schedule. The bottom line is that they are all going to be distracting. Added together, these little moments may lead to the danger of falling off your schedule!

What to do? When you get sidetracked or interrupted, you need to be aware of how much time is ticking away. Take that five, seven, or ten minutes into account while it's happening. This means to think to yourself that "Hmmm . . . four minutes already, and Bob's not to his point yet." Determine if the matter is urgent. If it is not, stop the conversation! Nicely . . . of course. You must take control of your time. Respond graciously and say, "Bob, I can see this is important. I want to hear the whole story, and I'm on a killer deadline.

Can we catch up on this later this week?" People will understand. If it turns out to be important, you'll hear the whole story. If it turns out Bob just needed to chat or vent, you've only lost five minutes of your time because you stopped him. Otherwise, you would've lost twenty minutes. Get clear on what interruptions you need to address and those that can wait.

Additionally, use the following tools and strategies to manage your time:

▶ *Use a calendar*—Plan your days and weeks. Mark out time for your meetings, project work, and other events on a weekly basis. Include a time buffer for potential surprises, distractions, and other unknowns.

▶ *Set priorities*—Rate your tasks, and identify what you need to do immediately, soon, and what you can leave for a later time.

▶ *Use technology*—Get a digital watch, phone, or electronic calendaring system that uses an alarm to remind you of important appointments.

▶ *Estimate travel time*—Give yourself enough time to get to those appointments and arrive on time.

▶ *Finish*—Complete what you set out to do.

▶ *Commit yourself*—Set aside blocks of time in your calendar to accomplish specific tasks.

 ## Knowledge

Knowledge is power. When you have the right information, you ask even better questions, make more informed decisions, and add value to your team and company. As a new employee, your job is to ask questions. The more you find out through your questions, the better your follow-up questions become and the more you learn. Start off on the right foot with the right knowledge. What kind of knowledge do you need?

1. Knowledge about your company
2. Knowledge about your company's industry
3. Knowledge that relates to your specific role and job responsibilities, that is, subject matter

Company Knowledge

Company knowledge is the information that's unique to your company. This includes its history, culture (why they do things a certain way), internal operations, strategy, and market share. When you have company knowledge, you have insight into how your company is organized, how various departments work together, and why there are certain rules and ways of doing things. It is important to understand the rules because it ensures that you operate within the limits and boundaries and not step on any toes in your first weeks on the job. Unknowingly crossing boundaries doesn't usually leave a very good impression.

Even if you are a maverick, companies expect that you will adopt their way of doing things . . . at least at the start until you gain enough credibility and respect. Get the essential company knowledge as quickly as you can.

Once you gain the knowledge, don't just sit on it. Keep your eyes open for opportunities to apply what you know about the company. For instance, you will be able to use your knowledge of the company culture to more effectively fit in or use your knowledge of the company's resources to help you quickly solve a problem.

Industry Knowledge

Industry knowledge means that you're looking at the entire business environment that surrounds and influences your company. For instance, if you work for a software company, you want to learn about the software industry; if you work for a clothing company, you want to understand the fashion and retail industries. Industry knowledge requires that you understand your industry's special language—the jargon. You'll want to know about your competition and the industry's history, and you'll begin to understand what leaders in your industry think are the major new trends.

It is critical to your success to have a strong understanding of the big picture. This helps you make more informed daily decisions. When you understand your industry, its trends and practices, and how your company fits within its industry, you can more effectively see where your job fits and where you can make an impact.

Subject-Matter Knowledge

An important component of the knowledge you bring to your job is having what we call subject-matter knowledge. This is the area in which you have expertise or experience. By having subject-matter expertise, you are able to ask insightful questions, make informed recommendations and decisions, and contribute your value to the company.

The knowledge you have should be treated as an evolving resource that you use and share with others. There are three methods of maximizing and managing this resource: Identify areas or subjects where you are knowledgeable, share what you know with others, and identify areas where you want or need to learn more.

A helpful method to begin to identify what you know is to define your knowledge using the following four categories:

- ▶ *Interpersonal Knowledge*—Includes understanding effective communication skills, relationship dynamics, and knowing how to work with different personality types
- ▶ *Professional Knowledge*—Includes areas of knowledge that correlate to a specific profession, training, or educational background that relates to your work
- ▶ *Special Interest*—Includes hobbies, education, or research
- ▶ *General Knowledge*—Includes a variety of disciplines including politics, history, cultures, languages, economics, and the arts

In your new job, you will have constant opportunities to apply what you know. As a new employee, it will be important to quickly demonstrate what you know by volunteering for projects or providing information or insight when you see an opportunity. Just asking an informed question, making a well-thought-out recommendation, or taking the initiative to be a part of a new project will quickly show that you have something valuable to contribute.

Once you have begun to identify what you know and how that differs from others, you can begin to share these distinct pieces of your knowledge. That's why they hired you. Don't forget that! When you share your knowledge, it ensures you make a contribution, builds your credibility, and expands your network of relationships with coworkers.

Balance what you bring to the table and what you think the company is open to regarding new ideas and ways of doing things. Companies can be very sensitive about that. Most people will come into a new company, be humble and not speak up about what they know for fear of being too bold; others come with the attitude that their way is the best way. Balance being open-minded with being opinionated.

 **Team**

"Brownnoser" is what some people think of when they hear the words "team player." We are not asking you to pretend to like those you can't stand. However, whether you consider yourself a people person or someone who likes to work alone, to succeed in your job, you need to understand how to play well with others . . . how to be a team player.

So if you didn't master playing well with others back in the sandbox, it's time for a refresher.

When you learn to get along with others, work is easier, more creative, and effective. From a purely practical perspective, to get ahead, you need to build relationships, credibility, and trust. If you are considered a jerk and tough to get along with, here are some things you can expect: Your team will make decisions without you, they will not support you in your decisions, or you'll be the last to know about things.

In this section, we are going to cover the two components of what it means to be a team player: collaboration and coaching. Being a team player is about having an attitude and exhibiting a set of behaviors that are helpful and well intentioned, regardless of whether you are part of a close-knit team that interacts regularly on projects or you work independently. You need to work well with others, even if you have an aversion to the "T" word.

Collaboration

Collaboration is about involving other people. As you explore and come to understand your new company, you will find that it is made up of different groupings of people. Depending on their size, these groupings might be referred to as divisions, departments, or teams. Company success depends on the ability of these groups to work together. Each department relies on others to deliver what is required. On a smaller scale, your ability to do your job well also means you need to collaborate. The more you invest in helping others succeed, the stronger the relationships you develop and the easier it becomes to call upon coworkers in the future. Collaboration can take on many different forms, from getting a coworker's opinion on your ideas to volunteering for a new project team or helping a teammate.

In certain situations, working alone gets the job done, but sometimes you will be more effective when you involve others in the planning and decision-making stages. Simply asking your coworkers for their input on one of your projects or ideas can create a sense of collaboration and demonstrates to others that you are inclusive—a team player.

Coaching

Coaching is about helping other people. A great way to contribute your knowledge, skills, or other resources is through coaching. Yes, you, as a new employee, can act as a coach! Remember, you are there to make yourself useful to the company. Your first step to coaching is your attitude and willingness to help. There are many opportunities to act as a coach. As you collaborate on projects, identify what you could teach that would be helpful to others. Sometimes beginning a coaching conversation is as simple as asking others how you can help.

A very important part of coaching others is making yourself approachable. Your coworkers want to know that they can come to you if they need help or have a question. Coaching others demonstrates that you are generous enough to invest your time in your coworkers.

 **Image**

Marshall Goldsmith, a top leadership consultant, explains that being professional is critical when someone enters a new environment, as opposed to being political or self-promotional. "I use the analogy of a Broadway play. The actors are always 'up and positive.' They dress in a certain way. It doesn't matter how they feel. They are not there for themselves. They are there for their customers. Even though they may have done the same play 1,000 times, this is the first time this customer has seen it. When I teach people how to change behavior, one of their concerns is being 'phony.' This concern tends to disappear when I ask them to focus on being 'professional.'"

Goldsmith offers a powerful and useful metaphor. The cast and crew do everything possible every single night to present the best show possible. There are no excuses. Among the dozens or even hundreds of people that it takes to put on a show there are always loads of personal problems: Dinner last night made me sick, I had a hard time getting a babysitter for my child, or the subway was running late. In a professional show, none of these excuses are ever even mentioned.

Your audience is the people in your company. They expect your highest level of energy and performance every day. No excuses.

A professional image requires that you develop "soft skills." (Don't be afraid, we're not asking you to hug a tree and sing "Kumbaya.") You can develop a strong professional image by doing the following:

1. *Networking:* Get to know others and thoughtfully build your network of contacts.
2. *Communicating:* Always be clear and concise, in person and in the written word.
3. *Personal PR and Marketing:* Send a clear message about what is important to you by developing a personal public relations (PR) message that communicates your image and values.

No matter what you know or no matter how good or capable you think you are at getting the job done, your ability to communicate and present yourself as a professional is crucial to your success. "But I'm comfortable at work in shorts and a T-shirt," says the manager of a high-profile team. Our response? You may sound smart, but all anybody is seeing is: "Shorts and a T-shirt!" In this section, we are going to cover the skills and subtle intricacies of identifying and crafting the right professional image.

Networking

The results you get from networking depend on the investment you make. Successful networking is more than just making contact and expecting rewards for your effort. Networking is about building relationships and expanding your network. Relationships take a lot of nurturing; you will need to make an effort to reach out to your coworkers to get to know them and share information. Let them know you are interested in the projects they are working on and offer your assistance or ideas, if appropriate. Networking fosters an open flow of information and assistance between you and your peers. When people have a need or exciting ideas or projects, they will think of you. You will be included and opportunities will present themselves.

Communicating

How many times have you heard about "good communication skills"? The job requirements stated good communication skills are a must. Are good communication skills really that important? Yes. Do most people do a good job of it? No. Effective communication skills are based on what you say and how you say it—in other words, your verbal and nonverbal communication.

Verbal Communication

Effective communication skills help you build relationships, get the resources you need, and give your coworkers confidence in you. Strong communication skills include the ability to:

▶ *Listen and understand*—Stay quiet, do not interrupt, and paraphrase what you understood.
▶ *Make distinctions*—Ask insightful questions to understand more of what the other person is trying to say.
▶ *Make requests*—Get clear on what you want and directly ask for it.
▶ *Communicate information or opinions*—Directly communicate your recommendations and suggestions.

When you effectively apply these communication techniques, you clearly convey your message to others and better understand theirs. Here are some examples of these skills in action.

- ▶ For your listening skills: "So it is important to you that we do . . . Am I understanding correctly?"
- ▶ For making distinctions: "When you say "customer," do you mean our internal or external customer or both?"
- ▶ For making a request: "So we've discussed needing to get a budget completed. Can I have your draft by Thursday afternoon?"
- ▶ For communicating information or opinions: "I agree with your recommendation, and before we commit, I have one concern I'd like to share."

Nonverbal Communication

Effective nonverbal communication is equally important. Nonverbal communication can reinforce what you are verbally saying or unintentionally send a conflicting message. For example, when you say "great idea" with your arms crossed and brows furrowed, you send a very different message than when you say these same words and lean forward with a smile. Regularly ask yourself "What message is my body language sending, and does it reflect what I am verbally saying?"

It is important to notice other people's body language and tone of the conversation. Is someone using sarcasm to be funny or not taking your ideas seriously? Does a furrowed brow mean the other person does not understand or does not like your ideas? If you notice unfavorable body postures when you are speaking, give your coworkers an opportunity to ask questions. Do not ignore their signals. When you acknowledge their body language by saying, "I notice that you are furrowing your brows, and I'm wondering if perhaps I am not being clear," you demonstrate that you are listening and paying attention to them.

Personal PR and Marketing

How do you know that BMW is considered the "ultimate driving machine" when not everyone has owned one? How do you know that Volvo has a great safety record when not everyone has owned one? Through marketing, of course!

A word, picture, or positive anecdote has been associated with an object and seen or heard by millions of people who have never experienced the product for themselves. When the association is believed to be true regardless of firsthand experience, that's good marketing!

You, too, have a product to market: yourself. You may not have an advertising budget; however, you are still responsible for promoting and managing your image. Let's call this your personal public relations for a professional image. With every contact, whether it is a phone conversation, presentation, or meeting, you are presenting an impression of who you are to your coworkers. Your effectiveness and success depend on how you are perceived. You have the opportunity to intentionally define yourself. If you aren't explicit about who you are and what you stand for, others will make assumptions and paint the picture for themselves. The intent of your PR message is to communicate your values and what you want to be known for to a broader audience.

To create your image, first determine what is important to you and what you want others to know about you. Next, demonstrate those values with the right behavior. Your words, actions, and look should all be aligned to support the image you want to project.

Craft and launch your personal PR campaign now because every interaction delivers a message. Say it, show it, and do it.

SAY IT: Get clear on what is important to you. Find a couple of key words or a phrase that captures your values and tell it to others repeatedly.

SHOW IT: The days of the anything-goes dress code are history. To be taken seriously as a professional, you also have to dress the part. Every company has a uniform, whether it's a suit-and-tie law office or a jeans-and-polo-shirt computer hardware manufacturer. Know your organization's uniform. Identify the uniform of your company's leaders. If you want to be a future leader in the company, dress the part. You will command more credibility and respect in a suit or slacks than in shorts or a low-cut top.

DO IT: Your behavior must be consistent with what you are saying and showing. If you are telling people that it's important to you that meetings start on time and you are usually five minutes late, you've just damaged your personal PR campaign, and it will take awhile to gain back people's trust that you value timeliness.

Remember: Say it, show it, and do it.

Put It All Together

Now that you've been introduced to the *5 Sink or Swim skills*, the next step is to jump in feet first. What follows is a 12-week guide in which you will practice and apply your new skills. For each week, you will be given a main objective. There will be specific goals to accomplish, skills to practice, and questions to ponder. *Sink or Swim* also provides suggestions for specific daily actions as well as reminders for what you should be doing each week with respect to the five concepts.

Keep in mind that the pace of your company may require that you speed up or slow down how you apply the content presented in the following chapters. This is your guide and a resource to help you succeed. Make it work for you.

By the end of the twelve weeks, you will have goals in place, and will have built foundational relationships, and have a comprehensive understanding of how your new company operates. Most importantly, you will have quickly positioned yourself for success.

A Final Note

These first twelve weeks in your new job are an important time in your life. You want to take extra care that you are minimizing outside distractions and ensure that you are setting yourself up for success. For instance, if you are a coach of a little league team, you will want to find a substitute for a while. If you normally stay out late during the week, you might want to change your routine and make sure you're getting lots of rest. This is your time and your opportunity to set the stage for what can be a fantastic career at your new company. Give yourself every chance to succeed.

Chapter 1

WEEK 1   Case the Joint

▟▊ Hi, my name is Pat. Today is my first day on the job. It took me three rounds of interviews with six different people, and they finally chose me. Two weeks ago my family took me out to celebrate. I took a few days off before starting my new job, and I'm excited and a little nervous. This could the best decision I've ever made or the worst. I was at my former job for five years and was very comfortable. Being the new person means in some ways that I have to start all over again.

"I want to make a great first impression. I want to demonstrate to my boss and coworkers that I can do the job they've hired me to do. But the first thing I need to do is get all the little things taken care of like tax and benefit forms and the bigger things like getting to know my new work environment. ▟▊

MONTH 1
• • • • •

MONTH 2

MONTH 3

Congratulations! This is your first day in your new job. Like all first days, you're probably excited and nervous. Maybe you even double- and triple-checked to be sure your alarm clock was properly set the night before. To make sure that everything is just right, you even paid extra attention to pick out the right clothes. The advice starts here: White sport socks and dress shoes are never a good combination.

It's amazing how much excitement and attention you put into your first day of work. Our goal is to keep you just as excited and motivated throughout the next twelve weeks and beyond. In this first week, focus on gathering information to better understand your work environment. Case the joint and figure out the lay of the land . . . literally. It's important to get those critical things that support your basic needs . . . like where the bathroom is, where to practice your modern hunter-gatherer skills (i.e., the cafeteria), and the emergency exits in case you realize this job is not for you . . . just kidding.

As you go through your first week, keep in mind the old adage: Knowledge and information are powerful, but having the right knowledge and information is power. If you have the right information at the start of your job, you have the power to make the best decisions during your first critical days at work.

Week 1 *Sink or Swim* Skills	Overall Objective: Take Your First Steps
Goals	Explore your new work environment.
Time	Establish your routine.
Knowledge	Gather information regarding your job and company.
Team	Familiarize yourself with your team and team processes.
Image	Observe the organization's culture.

Goals

What does it mean to case the joint? It means you are a detective, and your job is to figure out how your new company operates. While this may sound like an easy thing to do, it does take time to figure out the details of how your company works. In the first few days on the job, this information may not be readily available, or people may be too busy working on their projects to help you. Whether you have a welcoming committee or you are on your own, this chapter will provide you with guidelines to explore your new workplace.

Basic Survival Skills

In the wild, your basic survival needs are safety from jungle predators, food to keep you running, and shelter to keep you warm. Not surprisingly, the modern work environment is not that differ- ent. Let's start with the important stuff. We love to eat. We assume you do as well. Find the food source. It's easy to run yourself ragged, and before you know it, you'll need a boost to keep focused and sharp. When that time comes, you'll want to know where to go or if you have to bring food with you to work.

Find your workspace. It is your new shelter. Figure out who is in your neighborhood and be sure to introduce yourself. You shouldn't expect that they will bring over fresh baked cookies. It's incumbent upon you to make a good impression on your coworkers, not the other way around. After all, you're coming onto their turf.

Are you in a cube or an office? If it's an open space, how do voices travel, particularly yours? You don't want to inadvertently announce your arrival when your mom calls to see how your first day is going.

Be smart and know the exits around you. Just as with an aircraft, the closest exit may be right behind you. In the case of a water evacuation, your desk chair will not act as a flotation device.

Jungle predators . . . they do exist. They are likely camouflaged, come out at night, and occasionally show up at happy hour. No need to worry about them right now; just keep your eyes open.

Why Am I Here?

Good question to ask and answer in the first week. As you will find through the next twelve weeks on the job and beyond, there are employees who have become separated from their original career path and float around the corporate hallways. This is not you. A top priority for this week is to understand your job responsibilities, roles, and projects.

Part of answering "why am I here?" lies with your manager. Meet with him or her sometime during your first week. This will enable you to understand what's expected of you in terms of projects as well as expectations for the first few weeks on the job. You may have just entered a situation in which you are thrown directly into the fire and are expected to jump in and get started on a project immediately. You may have the luxury of having a manager who wants you to spend the first few weeks getting to know your new environment, the company, and your coworkers.

In case you cannot meet with your manager immediately due to scheduling, shoot for the earliest time possible, which hopefully will be in your second week. If neither the first nor second weeks are a possibility, there are still other things you can do to get going. Read on.

Outfitting Your Workspace

This is your home away from home. You want to make sure it is a functional environment that allows you to do your job with maximum efficiency. It is also a place in which you will spend a lot of time. Therefore, create a comfortable space.

Ergonomically speaking, ensure that your equipment is adjusted to your physical proportions. This includes such items as your chair, keyboard, and monitor. Spend a few minutes adjusting your furniture and equipment to ensure you are comfortable. Carpal tunnel syndrome is not your friend.

To get your workspace up and running, you will probably need an access badge, computer, e-mail account, and phone. Most companies operate on servers, and you'll need an account and password. Hopefully, this will have all been set up by the time you arrive. Since most companies are operating at warp speed, you may not have these necessities right away. You may find yourself having to march over to the IT department to convince them you are a new employee and to beg for a computer. No need to sweat it, even if you don't have these necessities on the first day, there are tons of other things you can do. Also, be mindful that while your company's lack of preparation for your arrival may seem disorganized or even downright rude, they may be testing you to see how you adapt. Do you proactively seek out the equipment you need or sit helplessly and twiddle your thumbs? Are you relaxed and accommodating, or do you throw a hissy fit because your (already) inundated colleagues didn't drop everything to make sure your workspace was wrapped up for you in a pretty red bow? Remember, your behavior is being watched.

A final thought . . . your cube/office space is a reflection of you. Does it say party central with Christmas lights in July, lava lamps, and shot glasses? Are you going for something more subdued as in no decoration or personal affects whatsoever? Decorating your space gives it a personal touch and tells people who you are. A word of caution . . . before you go crazy with disco lights, flashing neon, and poster art, take a look at how others have chosen to decorate their office and keep your décor within company taste.

 Time

During the first week, start off with the basics of time management: a routine. "Routine?" Some things in life should be boring, especially when it comes to getting to work consistently. It's important to establish a routine because it sets you up for success and minimizes surprises. Establish a routine that is consistent and predictable so you can manage your schedule.

Meatloaf on Wednesday Nights

Having a routine means bringing predictability into your work life. Although we are not advocates of weekly menu planning, it is important to have command of your schedule. Predictability allows you to be flexible if you need to make changes, because you readily know what your schedule can accommodate.

Your morning routine is critical to starting off on the right foot. Many people do not give themselves enough time and end up running out of the house with different-colored socks, no coffee, and a dog that's gone without breakfast. When you have a routine, you know how many times you can hit the snooze button and still get to work on time.

When you develop your morning routine, the best strategy is to work backward.

- ► How long does it take to get from your car to your cube/office and log on to your computer?
- ► How long does it take to get from home to work, accounting for traffic?
- ► How long does it take to eat breakfast?
- ► How long does it take to take care of other things like kids, pets, and/or spouses?
- ► How long does it take to get from bed to being dressed?
- ► What time do you need to go to bed in order to get a full night's sleep?

Before you know it, what you thought was a half-hour routine to get out of the house and on your way to work is really an hour, and you find yourself pulling up to the company parking lot at 8:55. What happened? Life happens. Make sure you account for distractions and interruptions. Give yourself plenty of time. Your routine helps you to accommodate last-minute events.

The same thing applies for leaving work. We are big proponents of work-life balance. You also want to ensure that you are giving the same attention to your obligations outside of work and being on time for your other commitments. This allows you to effectively manage the interdependencies between your time in- and outside of your job.

Recess Time

According to workplace research, smokers take more breaks, and the average employee is only productive five out of the eight hours they are on the job. We assume our readers are good for at least six hours.

As a part of your time-management skills, you will want to also observe how others take breaks on the job. You may be in an environment where breaks are mandatory and part of a very specific schedule. You may be in an environment in which breaks are a luxury and potentially looked down upon. Before you either take your 11:00 A.M. siesta or fill your bladder with the tenth bottle of water just so you can head to the bathroom for a break, understand the practices of your company.

Observe and talk to your coworkers. It's probably okay to take breaks if your coworkers invite you out for a cup of coffee or a quick casual chat. Some foolproof tips for effectively taking a break: Keep it short, get refreshed, and clear your head to get back on the job.

Standard lunch breaks are one hour long, but every company and department varies. Some folks may go out to lunch while others eat at their desk. Observe how your coworkers take their lunch breaks and the duration of them. If you have deadlines to meet, a two-hour lunch is not appropriate as your coworkers scarf down their sandwiches while typing away.

 Knowledge

Even though it's your first week on the job, it's a great time to start gathering critical information about your company. This week, start with the basics, such as industry information, company history, current products, and your company's future direction/vision. This foundational information will provide you with a basis for understanding your company and will later help you make the best and most appropriate decisions for your projects.

A traditional source of knowledge and information about most companies can be found in the new-employee orientation program. This gathering is typically a combination of personnel administration combined with company education. If this is available, you want to sign up for it. If a new-employee orientation is not available, you will have to do some research on your own to complete this section for the week. Augment the company's perspective by doing your own research.

The Big Picture

What is the big picture? It's the context for where your company is in its industry and how it will succeed moving forward. You have a stake in the game in this business. It's important that you have an understanding of what your company sells, how they sell it, and what goes into creating the products and services. More importantly, the big picture allows you to take into account the environment in which your company conducts business. Who is the competition? What are they doing to give themselves an edge? What is your company doing to stay ahead of the competition? Develop an understanding of the overall industry, including the past and forecasted trends.

Your understanding of the bigger picture means that on a daily basis you always know how the decisions you make relate to something larger. This includes everything from your hallway conversations to submitting a proposal for a new project.

Start by gathering information on your company's history. Look at when it was founded and what the founders hoped to create. Identify the first products and/or services that your company began selling. You will also want to track if and how these offerings have changed over time. If you want to get even more detailed, you may also want to look at what influences changed the direction of the company. A company's history can tell you a lot about how your company became what it is today.

Take a thorough look at your company's products and/or services. Read the Internet and intranet. Sometimes, larger companies offer a course intended to thoroughly introduce you to their products. Be sure to be knowledgeable enough about your company that when your friends ask, you have a solid answer. It would be awfully embarrassing at your next family dinner if Uncle Herbert proceeds to tell you about your company's newly released product while you cordially nod with a blank look on your face.

You will also find that your understanding of the company vision allows you to understand the direction the company as a whole is moving in and why certain products or services may be phased in or out. If available, get a company press kit. If your company is publicly traded, get the most recent annual report, which is usually available on the Internet. This will provide you with a good snapshot of the company's direction and performance.

Within your industry, determine the important players, their influence, and forecasted trends. Important industry players may include competitors, customers, and suppliers. Understand the influence of all these factors and what this means for the future of your company and its products/services. Continue to gather updates during your entire stay with the company and not just in your first week. Track events, industry news, and other important bits of information regarding your company on a weekly basis.

Welcome to Mars

You've started taking a look at the bigger picture outside your company including market forces, competition, and strategy. Now, come back down to earth and look at more specific knowledge about your company. Find out who's who before you unknowingly fight over the last piece of carrot cake with your company CEO. If you get a copy of the annual report, scan it for the pictures of company bigwigs. Review the company intranet and directory for the photos of company leaders. Get a copy of the organizational chart that lays out the various parts of the company, key individuals, and the reporting chain. This will help you understand how the various functions of the company are structured, and, more specifically, where you and your team fit.

It's only your first week, and you've started to wonder if you landed on Mars. What language are people speaking? What you are noticing is not just the result of today's modern, multicultural workforce. Your company is special. It even has its own language. Whether *Webster's* or *Oxford* agrees with its usage, it is a language nonetheless. You will find tons of acronyms that need to be deciphered, new uses of the English language, and a combination of words that have no meaning to people outside of your company.

As a new person, you are in luck. You can ask questions for clarification without fear of funny looks or reprisal for not knowing. Take advantage of it. Also keep in mind that company terms are invented daily. Even after ten years with the company, you may stumble upon a new "word." Make sure to ask for clarification. The last thing you want to do is agree to do something only to realize later that you did not understand what you committed yourself to.

 **Team**

Are you really part of a team? Sometimes, it may not feel like it. That's normal. In most work situations, you actually work in something called a work group as opposed to a team. The difference between being on a team and a work group is that the team is based on shared goals and accountability, while in the work group there are no interdependencies and your "teammates" all just happen to report to the same person.

Whatever the case, the importance of being a team player is transcendent. The benefits include camaraderie and sharing of ideas and resources. No matter if you are working alone, on a real team, or as part of a work group, employing team values will make you successful. It enables you to build relationships and accomplish more collectively than you would on your own.

Meet Your Team

Get out there and meet your team or, technically, those with whom you share the same boss. Don't hide out in your cube the first day and week you are on the job. You have the perfect introduction, "Hi, I just started. My name is . . ." Use it to your advantage to meet as many of your coworkers as possible. This will allow you to jumpstart your relationship with them. While they may not become your best friends, you still want a strong working relationship that will allow you to call upon their ideas and experience as needed.

"But I'm an introvert." Not good enough. Being an introvert doesn't mean you don't have social skills. It means you get tired from being around people and need to be alone to recharge. Unless you work in a North Pole observation post, you are going to have people around you. Your mission is to make contact. So get going and have fun!

What is protocol for getting to know your coworkers? First, sharing stories of what you did last night at the bar . . . hmmm . . . maybe not a good idea. It's appropriate when you first get to know a coworker that you share your past employment experience and give a verbal account of your resume with a tad of personal factoids (i.e., dogs, kids, spouse, housing location, etc.). Don't get too personal too quickly.

Remember, first impressions are everything; be professional, courteous, and curious. Don't just talk about yourself. Ask your coworkers about themselves. This is potentially rich information.

Meet Those Outside Your Team

Yes, there are people that exist around you outside of your immediate team. Get to know your neighbors. These relationships will increase your network of colleagues and the possibility of developing mutually advantageous and supportive relationships down the road; plus it's just plain courteous to say hello to the people around you. If you didn't believe it then, believe it now; it's all about who you know.

Organizations are social systems. This means by virtue of bringing people together for a shared purpose or simply gainful employment, you inevitably create an environment of interactions and relationships. When you know people and have good relationships, you are able to get things done efficiently and effectively.

Keep in mind that just because someone is not on your team does not mean you are not going to work with them at some point in the future. Furthermore, just because you are on a team does not mean that you will be interacting with your team all the time either. For example, you may be on a product-marketing team, each member of your team supporting a different product. You find yourself interacting more frequently with the engineers building the product you are marketing than with members of your own team.

Building relationships is part of your job. It helps you get work done more smoothly because you can call upon your network. Your relationships are also great sources of information. We cannot emphasize enough taking relationship building seriously. Make sure you join the team in all social events. This is particularly important early in your new job, even if you are an introvert. Attend the team dinners and lunches. However, pass on the alcohol. Jell-O shots are good fun, but are not recommended for work functions—even if they are social.

 **Image**

First impressions last. Your first week on the job is a significant period in which you make first impressions on your coworkers. It is important you focus on your image and how you make your initial impression.

During the interview process with your company, you probably made some observations about the company and its employees. As you prepare for your first week on the job, reflect on your initial observations. How did people dress? How did they communicate with one another? Was the environment quiet, or bustling and loud with activity? Keep these observations in mind before you bring back the "high five" as the new office greeting.

Look Around

As you pick out your clothes for your first day on the job, think back to the interviews you went through. Were people dressed casually or in a suit and tie?

Our suggestion is if people are in suits and ties, follow their lead. If others are dressed in a range of styles from very casual to formal business attire, find a middle ground between the two. This will allow you some room to adjust your style in either direction to fit the image you want. If after a few days, you find that people are more casually dressed than you are, a simple change in one article of clothing will allow you to make the adjustment with subtlety. When you dress down the middle, you have more flexibility as there will also be days when you need to dress up more for an important meeting. All you'll need to do is throw on a classic blazer or perhaps spruce things up with a tie.

Good grooming and appropriate attire are the basics of your image. Make sure you start with a "clean" slate. There is no reason to start off with a less than favorable impression, particularly when it is something over which you have control.

The Art of Casual Conversation

Your look is only one part of your image and the first impression you make. The way you talk and the kind of conversations you have in your first week are important components of the initial impression you leave. Notice how employees in your company talk to and greet one another. Is it casual and on a first name basis? Do you they shake hands every time, simply say hello, or give bear hugs? These are important things to keep in mind before you are overly demonstrative on your first day on the job. Greet coworkers appropriately.

Content
In this first week, keep your introductory conversations to surface-level information, such as your experience and few personal factoids, as previously mentioned in the Meet Your Team section. As

tempted as you may be to stoke the fires of watercooler gossip or form bonds quickly to ease social awkwardness, avoid the personal topics of hemorrhoids, your cousin's run-in with the law, and any recent alien visits you may have had. Keep your conversations warm, pleasant, cordial, and professional. The goal is to build relationships with coworkers, not scare them away.

Inquiry

The world does not revolve around you. In this first week, your focus is to case the joint and gather information. Be sure to ask others about their background, history with the company, and current projects on which they are working.

Volume

How loud do people speak? We doubt that everyone in the office wants to know what you are talking about at all times. This is especially true if you are in a cubicle environment. As much as we are proponents of knowledge sharing, your coworkers probably don't need to know what you want for dinner on Wednesday or need to hear your cell phone. Keep your voice and any personal effects such as radios and cell phones to an appropriate level.

Pace

There are two different aspects of pace in a conversation. The first is how quickly people talk, and the second is how quickly people move from one subject to another. Are conversations in your company rapid-fire drive-by or are they more lengthy and drawn out? Your speech pattern and ability to move from one topic to another needs to match your surroundings. You don't want to be too slow in a fast environment and too fast in a slow environment. Notice what's appropriate and adapt as best you can.

Length

The goal of the first week is to make introductions and have casual conversations. This means that your conversations may last anywhere from one minute to ten minutes in the hallway to a one-hour lunch. The length of the conversation should be appropriate to the setting. Remember the last time you got stuck in a conversation when you needed to be somewhere else? No matter how many hints you dropped, including looking at your watch, the other person still didn't get it? Do not make others a hostage of your conversations. Keep them to the appropriate length. Look for telltale signs that others are itching to leave and gracefully allow them to exit.

Your ability to start off with a strong impression in both your appearance and conversational skills will provide a foundation for others to want to build a relationship with you.

Put It All Together

Be your own champion! It is now time to put your ideas into action. The best way to learn is by doing. Take out your magnifying glass and set out to case your new joint. Figure out where you are and what you are doing. Gather information to better understand your company and begin to build relationships with your new coworkers.

Following is your calendar for the week. Plug in what you need to do in Week 1 to make sure you begin to case the joint. At the end of the week and before you get ready for a well-deserved weekend, take a couple moments to think back on this week. What went well? What did you learn?

Congratulations on completing your first week on the job!

Calendar for Week ① Day ① 2 3 4 5

Time	Action	Notes
6:00 A.M.		
7:00 A.M.		
8:00 A.M.		
9:00 A.M.		
10:00 A.M.		
11:00 A.M.		
12:00 P.M.		
1:00 P.M.		
2:00 P.M.		
3:00 P.M.		
4:00 P.M.		
5:00 P.M.		
6:00 P.M.		
7:00 P.M.		

REMINDERS

▶ Find the restroom.

▶ Find the food source.

▶ Find my office and make sure I have what I need for a proper office setup.

Calendar for Week ① Day 1 ② 3 4 5

Time	Action	Notes
6:00 A.M.		
7:00 A.M.		
8:00 A.M.		
9:00 A.M.		
10:00 A.M.		
11:00 A.M.		
12:00 P.M.		
1:00 P.M.		
2:00 P.M.		
3:00 P.M.		
4:00 P.M.		
5:00 P.M.		
6:00 P.M.		
7:00 P.M.		

REMINDERS

- ▶ Dress appropriately.
- ▶ Meet those who work around me.
- ▶ Make sure my morning routine is working to get me to work on time.
- ▶ Arrange meeting with my boss to get clear on role and responsibilities.

Calendar for Week (1) Day 1 2 (3) 4 5

Time	Action	Notes
6:00 A.M.		
7:00 A.M.		
8:00 A.M.		
9:00 A.M.		
10:00 A.M.		
11:00 A.M.		
12:00 P.M.		
1:00 P.M.		
2:00 P.M.		
3:00 P.M.		
4:00 P.M.		
5:00 P.M.		
6:00 P.M.		
7:00 P.M.		

REMINDERS

▶ Find organizational charts and company products/services information.

▶ Meet all teammates if I haven't already.

Calendar for Week (1) Day 1 2 3 (4) 5

Time	Action	Notes
6:00 A.M.		
7:00 A.M.		
8:00 A.M.		
9:00 A.M.		
10:00 A.M.		
11:00 A.M.		
12:00 P.M.		
1:00 P.M.		
2:00 P.M.		
3:00 P.M.		
4:00 P.M.		
5:00 P.M.		
6:00 P.M.		
7:00 P.M.		

REMINDERS

▶ Trim hair and nails.

▶ Identify alternative routes to get to work.

▶ Pay attention to appropriate pace, length, and content of conversations.

Calendar for **Week** ① **Day** 1 2 3 4 ⑤

Time	Action	Notes
6:00 A.M.		
7:00 A.M.		
8:00 A.M.		
9:00 A.M.		
10:00 A.M.		
11:00 A.M.		
12:00 P.M.		
1:00 P.M.		
2:00 P.M.		
3:00 P.M.		
4:00 P.M.		
5:00 P.M.		
6:00 P.M.		
7:00 P.M.		

REMINDERS

▶ Make sure all equipment for office setup is requested, if it hasn't been fulfilled already.

▶ Have lunch with teammate or coworker to build relationships.

Chapter 2

WEEK 2   Get a Firm Grip

▟▊ Last week was a blur. I can't believe the first week on the job flew by so quickly. It was great meeting everyone on the team, getting to know them, and learning more about the company. My computer is up and running, and I am looking forward to getting started on projects. But first, I need to clearly understand what exactly is expected of me. What are my specific responsibilities, and who else do I need to meet as part of my job? **▟▊**

MONTH 1

MONTH 2

MONTH 3

During these first weeks on the job you will be hard at work ensuring that you have what you need to make a positive impact. In order to set the right direction and demonstrate results, you will need to understand how your work correlates to your team's and company's goals. Defining these links will give you direction and motivation because it will enable you to understand how your job directly relates to your company's success.

Your objective this week is to understand the details of your job and how your role relates to the products and services the company delivers to its customers.

Goals

Your goal for the week is to get clear about your roles and responsibilities. Think minimization of ambiguities. The last thing you want is to jump into your work, only to realize that you misunderstood what was expected of you. Grab your life preserver! Meet with your manager to ensure you are both clear about what is expected. This meeting is an opportunity to understand your projects and help you define what success looks like—by your company's measuring stick.

Note: Depending on the pace and demands of your company and team, you may already be working on projects. Whether or not you have started on your projects, make sure you fully understand and confirm your role and when and what you are supposed to deliver. In today's competitive marketplace, most companies expect you to be a performer from day one—that is, they want a return on their investment of salary. Don't assume because you are new that you don't have deadlines and deliverables.

Week 2 *Sink or Swim* Skills	Overall Objective: Understand Your Job and How It Fits with the Rest of the Organization
Goals	Identify your key responsibilities.
Time	Adjust your daily routine to fit your needs.
Knowledge	Determine what you know and what you need to know.
Team	Identify the responsibilities of your team members.
Image	Practice your image skills by continuing to meet more people.

Hopefully, last week you were able to schedule a meeting with your manager to meet this week. In the event you cannot meet with your manager due to scheduling conflicts, draft an e-mail that provides an update on the following:

1. Your progress to date (i.e., orientation attendance, equipment setup, projects you may have started)
2. Any assumptions you have regarding your role, responsibilities, and priorities
3. Anything you might need to bring to their attention (i.e., requests or clarification)

The e-mail does not have to be complex; concise and to the point is sufficient. For example:

Hi Mike,

It's great to be here. I'm looking forward to working with you and the team. I'm sorry we haven't had a chance to meet. Things have been going great. I wanted to give you an update on my first week.

1. I've got my computer and phone system set up.
2. I attended new employee orientation.
3. I have a copy of my job description, and I'm beginning to identify additional details for my role. I want to confirm with you that I will also be expected to manage project code name Leprechaun. "By the way, the frosted marshmallows are in fact magically delicious."

I would like to set up some time with you as soon as possible, hopefully this week, to confirm your expectations and that I'm on the right track.

Regards,

Pat

No matter what type of working relationship you have with your manager, there are universal rules you can employ to make a strong impression and get off to a successful start. The most important is that your underlying objective is to make your manager's job of managing you as easy as possible. That starts with proactive communication.

Roles and Responsibilities

Hopefully, trumpets heralded your arrival at your new job. More often than not, only a few of your coworkers will know the specifics of why you were hired. It is extremely important not to assume others know what your role is.

Teamwork is part of corporate life, and teams are expected to collaborate. However, the downside is that job responsibilities between you and your coworkers can get fuzzy very quickly. While collaboration with your teammates is a good thing, it is also important to identify specific roles and responsibilities during a project. If there is something of interest that your teammates are responsible for and you'd like to try it on for size in order to learn, ask them first. Also let them know why you are interested. The more information your teammates have about your interest and rationale, the more likely they will be open to having you cross the border. The last impression you want to create is one of poaching your teammate's projects or recognition. The key to working together is to make sure you approach your teammates from a place of curiosity as opposed to imposition (i.e., telling them how it is).

Determine where there are overlaps with your teammates and where there are differences. This is important to know because you do not want to tread into other territory unnecessarily. You may find there is a tiger around the bend. People can be very territorial and threatened if you start to take over their responsibilities, particularly when it comes from the "new guy." Get clear on what your responsibilities are and how they correlate with those of your teammates.

Identify whether you need to partner with others outside of your team to accomplish your project goals. When you first meet with others outside your team regarding a shared project, be sure to reiterate your understanding of your role. This ensures you both are clear from the start. It also allows you to raise questions and negotiate if there are differences in opinions. Similar to the approach with your teammates, make sure you come from a place of being helpful, curious, and collaborative when working with others outside of your team.

Projects

Define the priority level of your projects. When you meet with your manager, make sure you understand the importance and priority he places on the various assignments and projects you are given.

Find out what success looks like for your project. This is particularly important because your vision of success may look very different than your manager's. After you understand that, you are ready to determine milestones. This is not a linear process. You start at the beginning by defining the objective and priority level, you then jump to the end to determine success factors, and finally you fill in the middle for how you get from where you are today to where you need to be.

Why does the middle (i.e., milestones) go last? Your manager may expect that you are the one to generate the milestones. He hired you to be the expert and to fill in the blanks. Conversely, you may also find yourself in a situation where you have a more "hands-on" manager. He wants to make sure you know the milestones and will dictate them to you or help you figure it out. Whichever the case, make sure your milestones are clear because you are the one who will need to deliver on them.

Pet Peeves and Preferences

As soon as possible you want to find out the preferences your manager has for how he likes to work with his direct reports. How can you find out? The easiest way to get this information is to simply ask. You'd be amazed how much people like sharing that kind of information. Additionally, it makes you look good for asking.

What specific questions should you ask? Think about it as the top-ten things your manager wants you to know about how to successfully work with him, including pet peeves and preferences. Pet peeves include dislikes, such as writing e-mails in all lower-case letters. For preferences, define the following:

- ▶ When you have updates, does he prefer e-mail, voice mail, one-on-one meetings, or staff meetings? What is her preference for the frequency of updates? How much detail does he prefer?
- ▶ When you need feedback on documents and completed work, does he prefer e-mail or meetings? What is his preference for the frequency of giving you feedback?
- ▶ When you have requests, does she prefer e-mail, voice mail, or meetings?
- ▶ When you have emergencies, what is the best way to get ahold of him? What does he consider an emergency?

Get into the habit of understanding what and how your manager expects you to deliver. When you understand what keeps your manager up at night, you are better equipped to prioritize your work effectively, make their life easier, and make them look good.

 Time

Whether you are a creature of habit or Miss Spontaneity, have an established routine. This will allow you to bring order and predictability to your days and weeks. Last week you began to practice establishing a routine for yourself. This week take it to the next level and revise and review the morning routine you established, and look at other areas in your work life where a routine might be beneficial. Incorporate a calendar system and task list to organize your work. A routine will help you accomplish your goals. If you need to, you can schedule in some spontaneity to spice things up.

Calendar System

Thousands of years of mankind's use of a calendar cannot be wrong. Whether you choose to use the Chinese, Hebrew, Roman, or ancient Egyptian calendar, just make sure it's the same as everyone else's in the office.

The use of a calendar system is your best success strategy. It enables you to organize your day, remember (and remind you of) your appointments, and prioritize. Although this is not a novel concept, we cannot stress enough the importance of getting into the habit of keeping a calendar. The calendar allows you to visually see your day and determine what can actually be accomplished given the various meetings and deadlines you have.

There's also another benefit to keeping a calendar. It provides you with documentation and reminders about what you have been working on. When the day comes—and it will—that your boss asks you what you've been doing over the last couple of months, you can review your calendar to refresh your now vacant memory.

Depending on the level of technology your company uses, there is a range of options. You can choose from sophisticated handheld devices to a basic paper-based organizer.

If you are already in the habit of keeping a detailed calendar, great job! Keep it up! If you are not in the habit, now is the best time to start. No matter what technology you choose, make sure it is the most efficient and compatible with your company's systems.

Besides putting your appointments and meetings in your calendar, here are additional tips.

- ▶ Put project deadlines and milestones in your calendar. This will keep these deadlines and key dates in front of you as a reminder to keep moving along on your projects.
- ▶ Block out chunks of time designated to work on your projects. This will help you plan to get work done and also allow for some flexibility should last-minute meetings arise.
- ▶ Review your calendar at least three times a day.
  - *At the start of your day.* Make sure you know what to expect and where to focus your attention for the day.
  - *Before you break for lunch.* Know what time you need to be back from lunch and what your afternoon looks like.
  - *At the end of the day.* Prepare for the next day and ensure that you are not surprised by the 7:30 A.M. meeting with the team in Europe.

Use your calendar system to start tracking how much you can realistically accomplish in a day, given your meetings and the unexpected things that occur. This will help you later as you take on more projects. You will have the ability to accurately forecast the time required to complete a project.

Be a Taskmaster

You can master your tasks, or your tasks can master you. Documenting and organizing your tasks gives you a sense of what you need to do. This keeps you focused as you check off one task and move directly to the next.

Your task list reminds you of what is on your plate and what needs to be done. Imagine your sense of accomplishment as you look back at your checked-off list of tasks. Since you kept a running task list that is now complete, you now have immediate feedback as you revel in the glory of all your astounding accomplishments for the day. Who says there's no reward in refilling the stapler (check), organizing your pencil drawer (check), and cleaning your keyboard (check)?

As you start to put meetings and deadlines into your calendar, you will find that you have some options for managing your tasks. There are calendars with an integrated task-list system, or you can manage your tasks the tried-and-true old-fashioned way of writing your list on a piece of paper, crossing it off when you finish, and transferring the list to a new sheet of paper when it gets too difficult to decipher.

Using a notebook is a great way to capture tasks that you identify as well as specific assignments. The notebook, whether it is in the form of a pad of paper or a spiral notebook, is a great way to consolidate your paperwork and know exactly where to find your task list at any given time. If you are a gadget geek, you can use your high-tech gadget to do the same. Let's be honest. As cool and advanced as your gadgets are, you can still write faster by hand, and your standard notebook doesn't run out of batteries or dump its memory. Whatever your choice, make sure it fits your work style, and more importantly, just make sure to keep a task list.

Observe Time

Now it's time to get a little personal between you and you. Don't worry; no one's looking over your shoulder. It's time for a heart-to-heart about how you think you manage your time and how you actually manage your time. Are you a secret slacker who looks really busy with a great, organized task list but doesn't get much done because you spend most of your time organizing? Do you procrastinate because you love the thrill and adrenaline rush of a quickly impending deadline? Do you freak out when you get an assignment and rush through it too quickly just so you can check it off your list?

No matter which of these types you are at the present time, you will become a master of time. Start by thinking about your time habits. Be honest with yourself. Think about the patterns you have already formed when it comes to starting and completing your work.

Identify which of your current time-management habits are useful. Keep using them. Now examine your darker side. Identify what does not work so well and does not advance your success. Determine what you are willing to commit to doing differently. Yes, it's like a New Year's resolution, except it's a new job. Modify your habits based on your reflections. If you need to slow down and pace yourself, do that. If you need to start a project twenty-four hours before the deadline date, start your projects sooner. Make the choice and start changing your habits.

 **Knowledge**

Now that you are getting a clearer understanding about the various components that relate to your projects and goals, it should become apparent which resources you need to get this work completed. In this section, think about what you are being asked to do and the resources you will need to do it.

Gap Analysis

The first step is to define what you need by way of a knowledge-gap analysis. What is a gap analysis? In the context of your goals, it is a method to define where you are, where you need to be, and what it will take to get there. A gap analysis identifies the skills, information, and knowledge you will need.

You assume that if you were hired for a job that you should have all the skills you need. While that could be true, there may be additional information or company knowledge that you do not have. It may also be the case that you made a job transition because you want to learn something new. Regardless of your situation, there is always new information, knowledge, and skills you will need.

To perform a knowledge-gap analysis, break it down. Define your overall job responsibilities and the projects you have been given. For each project, define the following.

1. What information do you need to get the job successfully completed?
2. What information do you currently have?
3. What information will you need to acquire?

Types of Resources

So many resources needed . . . so little time. As you've begun to notice from your gap analysis, there are a lot of different kinds of information you will need. The required information can vary from simple to complex. There are four different levels in which you can organize this information to help you develop a comprehensive plan to complete your tasks, acquire resources, and develop your skills.

LEVEL 1—Archival Information: This is quick hits of information that you can research on your own to develop an understanding in a particular subject area. This includes books, articles, research papers, and information available on the Internet.

LEVEL 2—People Information: This is information and knowledge that resides in someone else's experience or expertise. To access this type of information, first determine who these individuals are, make contact with them, and then retrieve the information. Because the information is coming from people, it is dynamic (not static like archival information). There are more variables such as accessibility, biases, and willingness to share that may also impact the kind of information you can retrieve and the time it takes to get it.

LEVEL 3—Training: It is a formal process by which you develop or increase your knowledge base and skills. Training can be in the form of courses available through books, online, or in classroom settings.

Training requires time and will usually vary from several hours to multiple days.

LEVEL 4—Certification and Degree Programs: An even deeper level of information and knowledge acquisition is through completion of a program in which there are governing bodies, specific requirements, and exams that ensure you know the information. This takes a longer amount of time to complete than training since there are credentials associated with these types of programs.

Use these four levels of knowledge resources to get clear about the kind of information you need to complete your projects and meet your role requirements. More often than not, the sources of information and knowledge you need for your projects can be found in the first two levels. Plan your deadlines and milestones accordingly.

 Team

This week you will continue the team bonding process by defining the goals of your team and the role of each team member. As you get clear about your specific responsibilities, you will need to understand what your team members are responsible for and how their role relates to yours. You will also need to ensure that you have a clear understanding of your team's goals.

Poke Around

Get an organizational chart for your department to get a better sense of how your team is structured. If you haven't already, make sure you meet each person on your team. Find out who they are, their role, history in the company, and the projects with which they are involved.

In the process of gathering information and learning about your team, you may be eager to announce to your coworkers your grand plan for making this the best year your team has ever experienced. Hooray! Go team! Your enthusiasm is great and is important.

Be aware that others may not share your level of enthusiasm. Each of your teammates has their own insights and opinions about how things work. Frankly, some of them might even be burnt out and in need of a change of environment. The last thing they want to see is the new person with their pompoms and big, bright ideas. Although you may see it as innocently sharing your enthusiasm and new ideas, you are still the new kid on the block. If you come on too strong and sound like a peppy know-it-all, you may ruffle some feathers.

Ease into your conversations. There will be areas where you have skill similarities to your teammates, and that can create a competitive situation, thus, the perception of threat. We highly recommend that you ask lots of questions. Err on the side of inquiry and engage your teammates with curiosity.

Look for opportunities to learn. Don't reinvent the wheel on a new project. If someone on your team has recently done something similar, get their wisdom and thoughts. Don't be surprised if you run into some territory issues or an initial unwillingness to share. Despite these potential speed bumps, it is still important to ask. To avoid initial resistance, share your intent: It is not to copy their work but to use it as a guide or template to quickly and successfully get work done for the team.

If you meet with resistance, contribute something first as an act of good faith. Share information or a resource you think may be relevant and ask for their input. Even if you don't have the right answers to start, when you ask for input, you are creating a reciprocal dynamic of sharing with others. Research has shown that people are responsive after they receive something from another person.

Keep the Love Alive

Now that you are becoming the social butterfly of the office, you want to make sure you build relationships that go beyond introductory meetings. Stay connected with people so they will think of you when there is a need or opportunity. Although we don't blame you if you would rather play minesweeper on your computer than send Bob in finance that interesting article on Sarbanes Oxley legislation. However, when you take the thirty seconds to reinforce the relationship with Bob, you are strengthening the connection and reinforcing your network.

To keep the love alive, we do not suggest you stalk your coworkers, fill their inbox with random e-mails, or send greeting cards saying "Thinking of you." Stay appropriately connected. When done correctly, you demonstrate to others that you pay attention to details in conversations and follow through. This reinforces your image and what you want to be known for.

Here are some ideas to help you keep in touch and build your network.

- ► Have lunch with different people on a regular basis.
- ► If you come across interesting and relevant information such as a news article, clip or copy it. If it is electronic, e-mail it to them.
- ► Keep a mental note of the last time you spoke to someone. Send them an e-mail to say hello, ask how they are doing, and, if appropriate, get together for lunch.

Your ability to be a team player is crucial to build a strong network of colleagues that you can call upon when needed. Your network is an invaluable resource. You will find that many people are quite lazy about networking, even when they know they should. Many people will often get involved and overwhelmed in their work, and they will forget to go back to their earlier connections to keep the relationship alive. Don't let that happen to you. Build your network at the start of your new job and keep it going!

 **Image**

As discussed in the Team section, it is important in your second week on the job to continue to meet people and build your network. It is also a great opportunity to brush up on and practice your active listening skills. That's right; every conversation is an opportunity to demonstrate your listening skills and contribute to the conversation.

Six Degrees of Separation

We are all connected in one way or another. No, we are not getting soft on you. If you don't believe it, do the statistics. There are really no more than six degrees of separation between you and any other person in this world. Even scarier is that there are likely even fewer degrees of separation between the people in your company and industry. Your industry probably feels like it is getting smaller every year; no, it's not just the mergers and acquisitions. When you are a strong networker, you'll find that you know just about everyone.

In your second week on the job, make sure you go out there and continue to meet people. Expand your network to include others in your department. You've met your team, and now there are others outside of the team with whom you should develop relationships. You may work with or for them down the road. They might end up working for you one day. Stranger things have happened.

Your network of colleagues can influence how easily you maneuver and succeed in the system. Think of your expanding network of colleagues as social lubricant: Knowing people helps get the job done faster, minimizes friction between organizations, and expands opportunities.

Although you are not expected to be thrilled by all of the people you work with, it is important, at a very minimum, to remain courteous and professional at all times. If you get upset, bite your tongue. If you receive an e-mail you find upsetting, take a deep breath and don't hit the "Send" button so quickly. Your reputation will get around quickly, and you want it to be positive.

Active Listening

What do you talk to people about when you first introduce yourself? Last week you shared your experience, background, and some personal factoids. You also made sure to ask the other person about him- or herself.

Although you may be the star of your show, you want to make ample space for costars. In line with the costar philosophy, it is important in your conversations to demonstrate that you are listening to the other person. While active listening is one of those overused terms in the soft-skill set, it is nevertheless such an extremely important one that even the bigwigs are not really good at it. So get a leg up on the competition and hone your active listening skills as you build your network.

Remember the basics of active listening:

- ▶ *Stay quiet when the other person is talking.* This is an obvious one, and so many people are bad at this. Close your lips if you must to keep from saying anything.
- ▶ *Do not interrupt the other person to get out a thought you have for fear you may lose the thought.* Interrupting demonstrates to the other person you weren't listening to them anyway because you were so deep in thought about some other issue that you just had to blurt it out.
- ▶ Look in the direction of the other person. In some cultures, it is appropriate to make eye contact; in other cultures, you only look in the general direction of the person. In both cases, it's not appropriate to stare. A soft gaze in the other person's direction is a good strategy.
- ▶ *Say relevant things.* Whether you follow up on the person's point with additional ideas or answer the other person's questions, make sure you stay on topic. If you quickly change the topic without a transition, the other person will clearly know you were thinking about something else while they were talking.
- ▶ *Use key words.* When you are unclear about what the other person has said, repeat back some of their keys words to determine clarification on a specific item. You won't look silly for asking. You demonstrate you were listening by repeating key words.
- ▶ *Paraphrase.* When you think you've understood what the person is saying in the context of the entire conversation, summarize in your own words what you've heard. This is a great way to have the other person understand that you have been listening when you can summarize major content areas discussed. Caution: Be sure not to do this too often in a given conversation since you will look like you are trying too hard or mimicking them.

Active listening is a core networking skill. These are simple and easy to follow rules. No one likes to talk to Joe, who constantly interrupts; Mary, who constantly talks about herself; or Barry, who goes off on tangents. Use these guidelines to have effective conversations.

Put It All Together

Be your own champion! Now is the time to put ideas into action. The best way to learn is by doing. Get a firm grip on your role and projects. Figure out what you are responsible for and what success looks like. Get clear on what information, knowledge, and skills you need to succeed, and put it all together on your calendar and task list.

Continue to build relationships with coworkers, specifically your teammates. Use your active listening skills in your conversations to develop a strong network.

Following is your calendar for the week. Plug in what you need to do in Week 2 to make sure you get a firm grip on what you are expected to do. At the end of the week and before you get ready for a well-deserved weekend, take a couple moments to think back on this week. What went well? What did you learn? What do you want to work on or accomplish next week?

Congratulations on completing your second week on the job!

Calendar for Week ② Day ① 2 3 4 5

Time	Action	Notes
6:00 A.M.		
7:00 A.M.		
8:00 A.M.		
9:00 A.M.		
10:00 A.M.		
11:00 A.M.		
12:00 P.M.		
1:00 P.M.		
2:00 P.M.		
3:00 P.M.		
4:00 P.M.		
5:00 P.M.		
6:00 P.M.		
7:00 P.M.		

REMINDERS

► Get clear on my role and project success factors.

► Practice my active listening skills, particularly making eye contact and not interrupting.

Calendar for Week ② Day 1 ② 3 4 5

Time	Action	Notes
6:00 A.M.		
7:00 A.M.		
8:00 A.M.		
9:00 A.M.		
10:00 A.M.		
11:00 A.M.		
12:00 P.M.		
1:00 P.M.		
2:00 P.M.		
3:00 P.M.		
4:00 P.M.		
5:00 P.M.		
6:00 P.M.		
7:00 P.M.		

REMINDERS

▶ Meet more coworkers.

▶ Determine key knowledge I need for my projects.

▶ Practice my active listening skills, particularly repeating key words.

Calendar for Week (2) Day 1 2 (3) 4 5

Time	Action	Notes
6:00 A.M.		
7:00 A.M.		
8:00 A.M.		
9:00 A.M.		
10:00 A.M.		
11:00 A.M.		
12:00 P.M.		
1:00 P.M.		
2:00 P.M.		
3:00 P.M.		
4:00 P.M.		
5:00 P.M.		
6:00 P.M.		
7:00 P.M.		

REMINDERS

▶ Find department organizational charts.

▶ Get my calendar and task-list system down.

Calendar for Week ② Day 1 2 3 ④ 5

Time	Action	Notes
6:00 A.M.		
7:00 A.M.		
8:00 A.M.		
9:00 A.M.		
10:00 A.M.		
11:00 A.M.		
12:00 P.M.		
1:00 P.M.		
2:00 P.M.		
3:00 P.M.		
4:00 P.M.		
5:00 P.M.		
6:00 P.M.		
7:00 P.M.		

REMINDERS

▶ Put deadlines to my projects.

Calendar for Week ② Day 1 2 3 4 ⑤

Time	Action	Notes
6:00 A.M.		
7:00 A.M.		
8:00 A.M.		
9:00 A.M.		
10:00 A.M.		
11:00 A.M.		
12:00 P.M.		
1:00 P.M.		
2:00 P.M.		
3:00 P.M.		
4:00 P.M.		
5:00 P.M.		
6:00 P.M.		
7:00 P.M.		

REMINDERS

▶ Practice my active listening skills, particularly paraphrasing.

Chapter 3

WEEK 3 **Buckle Down**

▦ Here I am in week three on the job, and I'm anxious to get going on my projects. I've got a pretty clear understanding of what's expected of me and what I need to do as part of my job. I still need to get more information from coworkers. I also need to schedule time with my manager to check in and ensure I'm on track. Hmmm . . . I better schedule this meeting sooner than later because her calendar gets filled up pretty quickly. **▦**

MONTH 1

MONTH 2

MONTH 3

Your broader objective for this week is to buckle down. This means you will get going on your projects and confirm your progress with your manager. You will continue to assess and practice your time-management skills and team skills and to polish your image skills by practicing when to ask questions, inform others, and stay silent. You are on track to your destination, and you want to make sure that life vest is securely fastened as you swim along.

Goals

Last week, you got clear on your role. In Week 3, you will get clear on your projects and what you are expected to deliver. This means you will think through the basics of defining goals for your projects. You need to be clear on the priority of the project, success factors, milestones, timeline, and resources needed. Although this is basic, we cannot stress enough the importance of having clear goals to know where you are going, how will you get there, and how you'll know when you've arrived. This is critical to know before you launch into your projects.

What Is the Goal?

You'd be surprised how often people realize halfway through a project that they are off course because they didn't clearly define the

Week 3 *Sink or Swim* Skills	Overall Objective: Get Going on Your Projects
Goals	Get clear on your deliverables.
Time	Identify the time frame that corresponds to each part of your deliverables.
Knowledge	Determine what resources you need and where they are found.
Team	Be clear on the expectations from your manager and team; network to get the information you need.
Image	Balance asking questions, providing answers and insights, and making clear requests.

goals of the project at the beginning. Sometimes the end goal can be a moving target. Before you dive in, make sure there's water in the pool. Look first and ask questions to make sure you are clear. When your goals are clear, your projects are more likely to be successful. Projects that cannot be executed on time, within the budget, and linked to a clear objective that supports the overarching department or company goals are likely to be scrapped—along with your position.

Success Factors

To be successful in your projects, start by looking at the end result. What do you hope to achieve? Take a look in your crystal ball and ask the following questions:

► *What do you see when you are done?*—What does completion look like? People often do not spend enough time asking about what success looks like. They typically jump into a project because it's something new and exciting or because of time pressures. When you stop to ask yourself what success looks like, you have a clearly defined goal toward which you can work. You will know when you get there because you've seen it before.

► *What will you hear?*—What will your manager, team, and client say about the project? Typically, after a project is completed, most people complain about how long it took, how complicated it was, or the silliness of the political maneuvering in order to get things done. As you define success for your project, think about what you want people to say about it when it is done. Do you want them to say it was fun and a great learning experience? If so, what do you need to do in your milestones and planning process to ensure that is what you will hear in the end?

▶ *How will you feel?*—What is the level of satisfaction and engagement you want by the end of the project? How can you make sure you are proud of the end product? Do you want to feel that you have learned a lot? When you get clear on the answers to these questions, you can work backward to ensure you get what you want out of the experience.

When you have a complete picture of success, you can more easily work toward it. This picture allows you to work backward and determine what needs to be in place from your milestones to timeline.

Milestones

If the success factors are the "what" you will accomplish, the milestones provide you with details on "how" to accomplish them. Your manager may or may not be "hands-on." Whether or not specific milestones have been identified for you, it is important to make sure they are clearly identified. Determine the smaller steps in the project that need to be taken in order to achieve the end goals.

Use your success factors as one of the means for helping you identify the milestones that need to be in place. For instance, if you have a concern that people may be upset by some of the changes you are planning, make sure you include several major checkpoints to ensure you have gotten input, support, and commitment to your ideas.

Resources

Given your identified success factors and milestones, consider the resources you need. This can include someone else's time and expertise, knowledge you need to acquire, budget, and equipment. It's a jungle out there, and resources are scarce. In order to successfully deliver your projects and accomplish your goals, you will have to clearly understand the critical resources you will need, how you will access them, and what you can live without. Be prepared to communicate why you need them in case your request for resources is challenged.

Once you have defined the resources you need, account for their availability. You may need to make requests of your manager and other colleagues for their time. Sometimes, your resources may take awhile to get. Can you still make your project deadline and goals without all the resources necessary? There may be times when you are expected to do your best to deliver on a project with limited resources. If this is the case, be sure to let your manager know so that the expectations for what and when you can deliver your project are renegotiated or fully understood. Scarcity is a fact of organizational life. Be clear on what you need, and don't whine when you don't get it. Remember to stay professional, be resourceful, and maintain a can-do attitude.

Deadline Dates

No healthy plan would be complete without specific dates. Add dates by working back from your end goal and the deadline date. Associate specific dates with each milestone. Consider the resources you need and if there are any timing issues because of resource availability. As eager as you are to show how quickly you can get something done, give yourself enough time, and account for the unexpected. It's always better to deliver early or on time than late. If you do not think there is enough time, you may want to show your manager your timeline and reset expectations. This may involve a renegotiation of deadline dates or even a reprioritization of your projects.

Time

As you work on your goals, actively use the time-management tools we've discussed previously. The tools are critical to help you stay on track and prepare for the uncharted waters ahead. Effective time management is not rocket science; it just takes a bit of discipline and a desire to truly make the most of your time. In your third week, you will identify the time frame that corresponds with each of your deliverables.

Use Your Calendar

Your calendar is not there to look pretty. It is for daily consumption. As we mentioned in earlier weeks, revisit your calendar at least three times a day.

- ▶ In the morning when you first start your day—this will help your brain get focused.
- ▶ At the end of the day—this will ensure you are prepared for the next day.

Fill your calendar with meetings, events, milestones, and deadlines. Throughout *Sink or Swim* you have tips, tricks, and suggestions to make the most of your time. Here are some additional rules of thumb to follow to effectively manage your time. Do not double book your meetings, and even worse, don't attempt to attend two meetings at once. This is the ultimate manifestation of multitasking gone bad. We've heard horror stories of individuals who've attempted to participate in one meeting by phone and one meeting in person. You may think it makes you an important person who needs to be in two places at once, but the impression you leave with others is that you are disorganized or clearly not respectful of other people's time.

Immediately update your calendar as events and work shifts. It is easy to get distracted, and forgetting to update your calendar can lead to a number of needless foibles. "The meeting with the CEO is scheduled for today!" If you carry an organizer, you can do your updating right then and there. Update your calendar regularly.

Back-to-back appointments do not necessarily set you up for time-management success unless you are very good at cutting off a conversation as you dash to make it to another meeting. These marathon meetings are intense, and you are expected to be "on" for hours in a row. The likelihood is that you will be running from one meeting to the next in a hopeless state of lateness.

Yes, there are times back-to-back meetings cannot be avoided. If so, be sure to let everyone at the meeting know you have a meeting afterward. It's important to you that you are on time, and you must leave the meeting at a specific time. No, you won't look like someone who thinks the world revolves around him, especially if you are explicit that it is important to you that you are on time for all of your meetings.

Task Lists

It's time to glory in the minutia: Your task lists will help take you down to a level of specificity you've always wanted and never thought possible. Here are the steps to help you get there.

1. Create and maintain a general task list of the major projects/items in which you are involved. This list helps you see the big picture at all times.

2. From the general task list, create a rolling task list. This rolling task list contains items you need to accomplish on a daily basis and gives you the flexibility to schedule other items later in the week.

    a. Put in your tasks for the day. This organizes your day and keeps you focused.

    b. When there are items that must occur later in the week because of availability, deadlines, or the fact that they are lower-priority issues, put them on the rolling task list for a later day. A later day could mean up to and beyond five business days. For instance, on Tuesday, some other tasks may come up that are not urgent and can be completed later. You can put it on your task list for the following Monday.

Here's how this all looks in application: You may be working on five separate projects, and the most important one will take one month to complete. When you break down the project into tasks, you realize there are certain items in the first week of the project that you need to complete by Wednesday and other items that can wait until Friday. Now you have a general and daily list that allows to you manage your time through the entire week and to project completion.

Beyond projects, your task list is a way to stay on top of all the things that need to get done: that document for your coworker, those follow-up calls, and review of that document your teammate requested. Your task list will help you knock out all those little extra tasks and ensure that your ability to follow through shows you are a star.

 Knowledge

This week your quest for knowledge will focus on the various resources you will need. Start with the resources that are available around you. Teammates and coworkers are a good source of information. As you begin to gather the necessary resources, it is important that you do a thorough job of identifying the people and information that impact your projects.

There is a good possibility that similar efforts might have been made by people within and outside of your company. It will be especially valuable to talk with people in your company about similar projects they've worked on, resources they can share with you, words of advice, and pitfalls to avoid. You will notice as you are working on your project that there may be additional skills that it would be helpful for you to develop.

Reinventing the Wheel

Unless you like to do more work, what is the point of reinventing the wheel? The efficient and effective way of getting your projects completed is to figure out what has already been done. No matter what you are working on, odds are that others have walked a similar path. It will save you and your company time, money, and effort if you identify and build upon existing work and resources. This can even inspire new ideas and ways of approaching a problem.

There was a reason we asked you to introduce yourself to your teammates and coworkers. It wasn't just to create a warm and fuzzy feeling. While Bob, Joe, and Mary may be interesting people though not necessarily the type with whom you want to spend your happy hour, they likely know things that would be useful to your project and overall integration into the company.

Don't be too proud to ask. There are tons of lessons and great bits of knowledge to be gathered from coworkers and teammates. Get insight on the subtle nuances they have figured out about how things get done in your company. This kind of knowledge only comes from experience, such as the little things that may upset the senior vice president's administrative assistant who controls his calendar.

As you conclude each of your conversations, make sure to always ask the following: "Is there anybody else you would recommend I should talk to about this?" No matter how dry a well your initial contact might have been as a knowledge source, they may have connections that will provide the information you seek.

Disclaimer: We are not asking you to plagiarize. Obey all patent, trademarks, and copyright laws. In addition, give your contributors credit. Publicly thank people for their knowledge and contribution. This is extremely important unless you want to quickly torch your bridges. You want to build trust and collaboration.

Develop Your Own Skills

Need to present your project plan in a few weeks but have rusty presentation skills? Thinking a degree in biochemistry would be great for selling your company's products to scientists? Although you may have gotten the biggest brain from your family's gene pool, you may start to find that there are areas in which it would be helpful for you to acquire additional knowledge and skills.

Your immediate priority is to define the short-term development you need as part of your current projects. Based on your gap analysis from Week 2, you should have a sense of exactly what you need. Determine if you need skills, information, or both. Identify what programs are available (internal and/or external to the company) and ensure they are timely so you can get the information you need as quickly as possible. Make changes to existing project plans based on any training you might need.

For long-term skill development, start a running list of the skills and knowledge you want to acquire. Refer to this list when opportunities to discuss your skill-development interests come up. These opportunities may be during performance review time or when you have your regular meetings with your manager. You will be prepared. Remember, when you continually develop your skills, you make yourself more marketable and valuable to the company.

 **Team**

As you may start to realize, a big part of taking care of business is building a successful foundation in your new job through relationships and effective communication. In this section, look at ways to reinforce interdependent relationships, specifically with your manager and teammates.

Update your manager. As mentioned in the earlier section in this chapter on goal setting, various changes may occur to your projects from changing scope to a different end goal. For these reasons, it is important to ensure you are on track. As you identify these changes to your project, keep your manager updated. You will also want to be in touch with your teammates. They have valuable insights into both the content of your projects and the process by which to expediently get work done.

Managing Your Manager

You mean you get to manage your manager? Absolutely, it's a must. As counterintuitive as that may sound, there is an underlying expectation that you will be one step ahead of your manager when it comes to your work. The goal for any manager is to have a direct report that is a mind reader.

Here are some examples of what it means to manage your manager. It means you are self-sufficient and do not need a lot of hand-holding. You anticipate your manager's every need by coming to the table prepared. For example, in meetings, you go in prepared with an agenda and key items you want to discuss. You invest the five to ten minutes to develop an agenda that keeps you and your manager on track and focused. Finally, managing your manager means you provide the right information at the right time. A key part of this is to understand her preference for updates and meetings.

Umm . . . There's Something I Need to Tell You

Surprise! No one wants to be blindsided. It's never a fun experience when you don't see something coming. It's like getting dumped by your ex. There were no signs that they couldn't stand the way you chewed your food. Your manager is no different. They need critical information on a regular and timely basis to make adjustments and decisions as necessary. Updates ensure your manager knows what is going on so that she has an answer when asked by her own manager.

Get into the habit of providing updates that include what is going well, as well as the challenges you may be facing. Provide your own recommendation before you ask for your manager's suggestions to address a challenge. This demonstrates you are thinking ahead and contributing value to the team. Although your manager may be a very busy person, it is still important to provide updates by e-mail or voice mail, even if you don't get a response from them.

Avoid the practice of communicating with your manager only when there is an issue. If you continue this practice, they will associate you with problems. There are other less desirable conclusions they can draw, such as you are not well equipped to do the job. To ensure a positive image in your manager's mind, provide your updates with overall project status. This includes what is working well, what isn't, plans to address these challenges, and, if needed, requests you have for your manager's assistance.

Build upon your work in the previous week. You were asked to determine the best way to communicate information with your manager. Based on your understanding and our recommendations for the content of your updates, determine what you need to communicate and when best to provide your manager with the status of your projects this week.

Why Meet with Your Teammates?

As mentioned in the knowledge-management section, your teammates hold valuable information about the ins and outs of getting work done. Build upon their knowledge and avoid the pitfalls they have encountered.

Sounds great on paper . . . what if they don't want to share? One of the challenges of being the new person on the team is that you may be perceived by your teammates as a threat. Though few may acknowledge this, it's true. Think about the last job you had and when the new person started. Didn't you have a nagging concern that she might upset the gentle balance on the team? Specifically, there was a possibility that she might've upstaged you and others. These are natural concerns.

Now that the shoe is on the other foot, be sensitive to how your teammates might perceive you. Instead of announcing big plans with the utmost enthusiasm and confidence, first build relationships by asking questions and learning about their experience and team history. Minimize any kind of concerns your teammates may have about you. The quicker you build trust, the better. Building trust by asking others about their experience is a great way to start. It shows that you are interested in learning. Although there may be a few who are suspicious and paranoid, don't take it personally. It is still okay to ask, especially since you are new.

 **Image**

Have you ever walked away from a meeting with a feeling that you didn't quite understand what just happened? You were talking; others were talking . . . you thought you were listening. Only now you realize that you can't remember what exactly was conveyed by anyone. In retrospect, people were talking over each other, and no one was truly listening. Everyone was just waiting their turn (or not) to state their opinion.

Successfully building and conveying your image is dependent upon effective communication. In this section, you will build upon your listening skills from Week 2 and refine your ability to ask questions and state your opinions. You will also refine your phone and e-mail communication etiquette.

Give and Take

Think back to the last great conversation you had. Specifically, the last great work conversation you had. It may have been in a staff meeting or a one-on-one meeting with a colleague. More than likely, it was a conversation in which your views and opinions were taken seriously and perhaps you learned something from others as well. It was a conversation that felt equitable. The other person probably walked away with similar feelings. So what made it so great?

Ideally, conversations are an exchange of questions, opinions, and statements of fact. The art of effective conversation is a fluid display of each party's opinion and genuine curiosity expressed between people. This often does not happen in the workplace. Most people are too busy to ask for your thoughts and simply make requests or bark their opinions. This method of communication is often frustrating for many people. The result can be a sense of not being heard or feeling that information is not clearly exchanged. Fortunately, you can control how you engage with others, and you can influence how others communicate with you.

The objective of all conversations is to convey information. Ensure that your conversations are as effective as possible. It is your job to make sure you ask the opinions of others and state your own. When there is a balance, you have a greater flow of information. As we know, information is power. Effective conversations open up the flow of information.

What exactly is the skill of effective conversation? It is a balance of asking questions and stating opinion. The nature of a relationship determines the sequencing of opinions and questions. As stated earlier in the Team section on managing your boss, you first want to state your opinion and then invite questions. The reason for this is because your boss is expecting you to tell her your recommendations and thoughts on how to solve an issue. That is why they brought you into the company. If you are shy about stating your opinion, get over it. Furthermore, if you do not state your opinion, your manager and others may perceive you as potentially not interested or, worse, insecure. Make sure you project the image of confidence and success.

When working with peers, it is important that you start off by asking their opinion and then stating your own. The rationale is the same as when you and another individual come upon a doorway at the same time. It is simply polite to let the other person go first. In the case of peers, you do not want to alienate them or look like you are upstaging them. Keep in mind that you are not just asking them for their opinion to be polite. The information you get might change your opinion or redirect your initial inquiry.

In the case where you have direct reports, you want to make sure you ask the direct reports for their opinion first. Due to power dynamics (i.e., you are the authority figure), you want your direct reports to openly give their opinion without being intimidated by yours. These principles are important to follow if you want to master the art of effective conversation and build a strong image in your company.

Often you will find yourself in conversations with others who may be a bit stunted in their communication aptitude. Perhaps you may have a manager who can only give orders or a coworker who seems to talk forever without truly making a point. No matter what the situation, your objective is always to be professional and to exchange enough information to be successful. In tough situations, ask probing questions to get clarity. Once you get enough information, leave the situation as quickly as possible. If needed, check your sanity with a trusted coworker or colleague outside of the company.

Make Clear Requests

Remember the time you hinted at wanting a bracelet for your birthday and instead got a wallet? Not quite what you wanted as you tossed the wallet into the back of your closet never to be seen again. Yes, sometimes in life your hints don't get heard. In the work-place, you cannot afford to have this happen. You can't always rely on subtle hints. Communicating who you are and what you need for your success requires clarity and confidence.

The objective of making clear requests is to ensure that you are effectively communicating what you need to the people around you. Being up front may not be the easiest communication skill to develop. Many people avoid confrontation or may not feel comfortable at the thought of asking for things from others. An effective, clear request is polite and thoughtful, and communicates not only the specifics of your request, but also why you are making the request.

Effectively making clear requests requires a bit of balance between humility and boldness. For those of you who avoid or never learned to ask for things, it's time to learn. You need to get over this if you are to be successful in the workplace. On the other end of the spectrum, if you are one of those individuals who are not shy about asking and are perhaps even a little demanding, you need to soften the blow.

When you make a request, have the following components in mind so you are being as clear as possible:

▶ *Who*—who are you making the request of? In team meetings, you may throw out a request, everyone agrees it's a good idea, and no one owns the idea.
  - *Poor request:* "How about if we got additional data for our client?"
  - *Strong request:* "Joey, will you get additional data for our client?"

▶ *What*—what exactly are you asking for? You may be clear on what you want. Are you being as explicit as possible?
  - *Poor request:* "Joey, will you get additional data for our client?"

- *Strong request:* "Joey, will you get the last five years' net and gross revenues for our client?"
▶ *When*—when exactly do you need the information? You may think the situation is urgent, and the other person have no idea you are waiting for them. Be clear on what the time frame is. That is most helpful to others.
  - *Poor request:* "Joey, will you get the last five years' net and gross revenues for our client?"
  - *Strong request:* ""Joey, will you get the last five years' net and gross revenues for our client by Tuesday?"

When you are clear about what you are asking for, you increase the likelihood that you will get the information you need when you need it. Work gets done through a series of requests. Someone at the top, for example, the president, makes a request of one of her vice presidents to get an idea going. The vice president then turns around and asks their managers to get a team of people together to get started on the project. The managers then turn around and ask their teams to do the work. As requests are being made, the work that gets produced increases. Remember, you want to make requests to initiate work (i.e., requesting a meeting to gather more information), and you also want to be clear and forthright.

E-mail and Phone Etiquette

We have been talking the last couple of weeks about ways you present yourself at work verbally (i.e., ask questions and state your opinion) and nonverbally (i.e., dress code). It is worth noting that e-mail and phone communication are different venues in which to apply the skills you have learned. In today's workplace, most communication takes place virtually, either over the phone or via e-mail. Although virtual communication can speed the communication process, there are also some potential pitfalls.

Let's start with phone etiquette. The following are tips and suggestions for making sure you are professional and cordial on the phone.

▶ *Don't answer the phone if you can't talk.* Let it go to voice mail instead. The understanding is that if the call goes into voice mail, you are neither available nor at your desk. That's the point of voice mail.

▶ *Don't talk loudly.* Whether you are in your cubicle, office, or on your cell phone, there is less likelihood that you can be heard if you speak at a lower volume. Plus it is inconsiderate to assume that your conversation is so important that it needs to be broadcast to everyone within twenty feet of you.

▶ *Leave short and clear voice mails.* Two minutes is too long to listen to a voice mail. Cryptic voice mails such as "It's me, call me" do not provide the other person with adequate information or increase the likelihood they will be pleased to return your call. State who you are, the nature of your call, and where you can be reached.

▶ *Follow up within twenty-four hours.* When someone leaves you a voice mail, call or e-mail them back to respond, even if it is to acknowledge that you will address the issue at a later time.

With the high reliance on and use of e-mail, it is important that your e-mail etiquette be up to par. The assumption with e-mail is that you have time to think about your response before immediately hitting the "Send" button. Furthermore, because it is written communication, it serves as documentation of a conversation. In many instances, this can work to your advantage for future reference and later reading. In other instances, it can be a huge source of embarrassment when it gets passed around by colleagues.

▶ *When drafting an e-mail, double-check your grammar and spelling.* Most e-mail systems have a spell-checker program. Use it. Read your e-mail a minimum of twice if you are in a hurry and use a standard of three times to make sure you catch everything before you send it. Read it slowly and out loud if you have a tendency to make a lot of mistakes.

▶ *Wait until you calm down before you send angry e-mails, which will come back to haunt you.* Anger will show up in the tone of your e-mail. Never use all capital letters, which is quite annoying to read. It also indicates you are upset and out of control. This is not appropriate in a professional environment. Others assume you had time to think about the issue, lower your blood pressure, and come across as professional. If in doubt, get a perspective check from a trusted colleague who can read through a draft and tell you if your tone or wording is harsh or inappropriate.

▶ *Don't send out gratuitous e-mails at 9:00 P.M. at night.* Many corporate employees have been regular recipients of "the look at me I am still working at night e-mail." Unless it is in conjunction with a project or deadline, it generally fails to impress. If anything, it demonstrates poor time management and a need for a life outside of work, unless you work an alternative schedule. It may even look like you are creating busy work for yourself, which begs the question of what you are doing during the daytime when you should be working.

▶ *Follow up within twenty-four hours.* Similar to voice mail, it is important that you get back to people within twenty-four hours and give them a projected time if you cannot complete their request. This process also ensures that you do not get behind with e-mail. It is very easy to go from 100 e-mails daily to 500 e-mails by the end of the week, if you are not keeping up with your e-mails.

These are simple and easy tips to maximize your efficiency and professionalism on the job. How you communicate with others sets the stage for how you are perceived. There is nothing more important than ensuring that what and how you communicate intentionally supports the image you want to project.

Put It All Together

The best way to learn is by doing. Buckle down and get going on your projects. Get the resources you need and meet with the people that can help. As you get the work going, ask your teammates for information and use it as an opportunity to build trust and practice communication skills.

Following is your calendar for the week. Plug in what you need to do in Week 3 to make sure you buckle down and get going on your projects. At the end of the week and before you get ready for a well-deserved weekend, take a couple moments to think back on this week. What went well? What did you learn? What do you want to work on or accomplish next week?

Congratulations on completing your third week on the job!

Calendar for Week ③ Day ① 2 3 4 5

Time	Action	Notes
6:00 A.M.		
7:00 A.M.		
8:00 A.M.		
9:00 A.M.		
10:00 A.M.		
11:00 A.M.		
12:00 P.M.		
1:00 P.M.		
2:00 P.M.		
3:00 P.M.		
4:00 P.M.		
5:00 P.M.		
6:00 P.M.		
7:00 P.M.		

REMINDERS

▶ Track your milestones to make sure you are making progress. Note where you have questions and concerns.

▶ Meet with your manager to discuss progress, questions, and recommendations for solutions.

▶ Make clear requests of others to get your work going.

Calendar for Week ③ Day 1 ② 3 4 5

Time	Action	Notes
6:00 A.M.		
7:00 A.M.		
8:00 A.M.		
9:00 A.M.		
10:00 A.M.		
11:00 A.M.		
12:00 P.M.		
1:00 P.M.		
2:00 P.M.		
3:00 P.M.		
4:00 P.M.		
5:00 P.M.		
6:00 P.M.		
7:00 P.M.		

REMINDERS

▶ Put all of your deadlines and milestones on your calendar.

▶ Create and use your daily task list.

▶ Schedule meetings with teammates to discuss their experience and advice.

Calendar for Week ③ Day 1 2 ③ 4 5

Time	Action	Notes
6:00 A.M.		
7:00 A.M.		
8:00 A.M.		
9:00 A.M.		
10:00 A.M.		
11:00 A.M.		
12:00 P.M.		
1:00 P.M.		
2:00 P.M.		
3:00 P.M.		
4:00 P.M.		
5:00 P.M.		
6:00 P.M.		
7:00 P.M.		

REMINDERS

▶ Balance asking good questions and offering your opinion.

▶ Check your e-mail etiquette. Get back to people on time.

Calendar for Week ③ Day 1 2 3 ④ 5

Time	Action	Notes
6:00 A.M.		
7:00 A.M.		
8:00 A.M.		
9:00 A.M.		
10:00 A.M.		
11:00 A.M.		
12:00 P.M.		
1:00 P.M.		
2:00 P.M.		
3:00 P.M.		
4:00 P.M.		
5:00 P.M.		
6:00 P.M.		
7:00 P.M.		

REMINDERS

▶ Leave clear and short voice mails.

▶ Identify areas for you to develop additional skills immediately and down the road.

Calendar for Week ③ Day 1 2 3 4 ⑤

Time	Action	Notes
6:00 A.M.		
7:00 A.M.		
8:00 A.M.		
9:00 A.M.		
10:00 A.M.		
11:00 A.M.		
12:00 P.M.		
1:00 P.M.		
2:00 P.M.		
3:00 P.M.		
4:00 P.M.		
5:00 P.M.		
6:00 P.M.		
7:00 P.M.		

REMINDERS

▶ Read and reread your e-mails to make sure they are grammatically correct and state what you intend.

▶ Create your task list for next week.

Chapter 4

Immerse Yourself

▌▐Boy, am I glad I had that meeting with my manager last week. She really helped me to identify the people I need to talk with to move my projects along. It felt good to start doing the work that I was hired to do. I got interrupted a lot last week with tons of odds and ends. I'm really looking forward to making more progress this week, especially meeting with the people my boss made reference to. Luckily I was able to get on their calendar this week. ▌▐

MONTH 1

MONTH 2

MONTH 3

Are you swimming yet? By now, you are making progress in your new work environment. In this week, you will draw upon what you have learned and move forward to immerse yourself in your projects. By now, you've been on the job for just about one month, and you're doing the work you were hired to do. But before you get swept away, continue to take in new information, keep pace, and make adjustments to stay on course toward success.

Goals

Surprise! "They actually want me to do things around here." Yes! Unlike your previous job where they might've paid you good money to practice the art of laying low, looking busy, and the three-hour lunch, this job has plans for you. Rise to their expectations and make a great impression in your first twelve weeks and beyond; keep the momentum going!

As you immerse yourself in your projects, you may realize that the plans you initially drafted may need to change as a result of new information, changes in larger team objectives, or other influences. In this week, you are going to continue to stay in the flow of your work and at the same time review your projects and make sure you are on track. Successful project management is a combination of planning, implementation, and continually reviewing your plans to ensure you are on track.

Week 4 *Sink or Swim* Skills	Overall Objective: Stay on Track with Your Plan
Goals	Make progress in your work.
Time	Plan for interruptions in your work week.
Knowledge	Tap into relevant knowledge resources.
Team	Begin to share your resources with your team.
Image	Build rapport and trust.

Man with a Plan

You don't want to fall into the trap of overplanning. Among the collection of office characters, cast your attention to someone we will name the "Planner." Every time the Planner walks into the room, everyone rolls their eyes because they know what the Planner will say: "I haven't started yet, I'm still planning out the details." As important as good planning is, actions speak louder than words.

In this week, if you haven't already, get down to action. Ironically, it's not until you are steeped in a project that you realize your plan might need modification. C'est la vie! Change is to be expected and welcomed. Fortunately, you are ready to adapt your work to new demands because your eyes are open to new information and you expect that changes will occur. Think Gumby…flexible, adaptable, and likable.

Check Your Milestones

The effective project planner always ensures that they are on course by reviewing their milestones on an ongoing basis. Now that you've begun to work on your projects, take a little bit of time to ensure the milestones you've laid out still take you down the path of success.

As you work on your projects, you may realize that there is added complexity or, if you are lucky, greater simplicity in the steps required to complete a project. Scan your milestones to see if you need to add more details or collapse multiple milestones into one or two. Also, ensure that the resources needed to accomplish each milestone are the same. New milestones might require new or additional resources. Build into your plan any additional resources required and the steps to get to those resources.

Scope Creep

Remember back to the last time you moved. Before you began to pack up and order the truck, it didn't seem like there was too much stuff in your house. You figured it would take a total of six hours to move. Then moving day came, the movers were there at 8:00 A.M., and they didn't leave until 7:30 P.M. at night. You were charged for overtime. Things just keep appearing. Boxes and furniture just kept showing up.

Well, your projects are no different. Often you'll find yourself in the middle of a project that you thought had a clearly defined destination, goals, and measures of success, only to realize you are now cast adrift in a sea of ambiguity. This is "scope creep." Things might have seemed so clear just days before, but now you have a queasy feeling that the project has changed. These changes can be subtle and sneaky or big and bold. Symptoms of "scope creep" include increasingly vague goals and additional objectives that don't relate to the project's initial desired result.

To avoid "scope creep," do the following:

1. Ensure you have clearly defined project goals.
2. When you get the sinking the feeling that your project is off course or that coworkers are adding work, communicate your observations that the original objective appears to be changing.
3. Renegotiate when you notice that your project scope is changing.

An additional symptom of "scope creep" is when other projects get added to yours. These add-ons are often orphan initiatives that were abandoned, never quite got off the ground, or were never formally terminated. As adorable as these orphan initiatives can be, once they attach themselves to your projects, they can become burdensome parasites. Keep your eyes open and stay clear on your project objectives. Knowing what your project needs will help you differentiate between valid additions and an orphan looking for a home.

Same Target?

What does your project have in common with a backyard birthday game of bashing open a piñata? Like a piñata your project objectives have the potential to become moving targets. As "scope creep" relates to a project's changing size, moving targets are destination issues. With moving targets, sometimes a goal changes without your even knowing.

If you think your target is starting to move, take a look at the larger plan you've laid out. Confirm with teammates or your manager that the end goal is still the same. The most valuable tools you can have for these situations are your observations and speaking up when things have changed. Like "scope creep," if your destination has changed, go back and renegotiate your deadline dates and what you are expected to deliver.

Make sure you speak up and test your observations. Although this may feel like you are being a squeaky wheel and perhaps challenging others or the system, it is your responsibility. We are not suggesting you run around and scream bloody murder for the change that's occurred and point a finger at the first person you can find to lay blame. Instead, inquire politely with a tone of curiosity and civility that you thought you were expected to deliver X and now it looks like Y. Is that an accurate assessment? If so, you need to reprioritize some items on your project list to accommodate the change or even renegotiate the deadline.

Yes, you may get upset at the thought of redoing your Gantt chart, and your frustration may not be mitigated through cordial discourse and inquiry. However, there is not much else to say than get over it, break out Mr. Squeeze, the stress-release grip doll, and move on. Change is a natural part of the work environment.

 Time

As you work through your fourth week on the job and immerse yourself in your work, you will find that there are plenty of distractions. Keeping your projects on track and delivering on daily demands will require that you effectively balance your plans with the potential for the unexpected. To strike this balance will require you to review how your time-management skills are shaping up. Specifically consider if your daily and weekly planning take into account the potential for diversion.

Right Place, Right Time

Self-reflection time! Don't roll your eyes. Be honest with yourself. What have you noticed over the last decade and more specifically in the last several weeks about how you manage your time? Are you managing your time effectively? Are you feeling stressed out every morning as you sit in traffic hoping no one in the office notices you're late for the 9:00 A.M. staff meeting? It's time to break the cycle.

In this week, review your time-management skills to make sure you get to your appointments on time. In fact, try something even better; get to your destinations five minutes early. Imagine the benefits of arriving five minutes early to each meeting. You'd have more time to get settled. You'd be less stressed. It would also give you a few moments of quiet time to think about your next task, organize your task list, or catch up on some quick notes or e-mails (if you carry your laptop or PDA with you). Think about it; you could even save time by being early.

Think back through the last three weeks. Have you been early, on time, or late? What do you want your timing to be, moving forward in the next nine weeks and beyond? When do you want to arrive at work and at meetings? By what time do you want to be home? How tight do you want your deadlines?

Some of you may decide that you like procrastination and the coinciding adrenaline rush. While that may be okay for you, make sure it does not impact anyone else and that it does not cause you too much stress. Be aware of the reputation you develop. If others find out you like to procrastinate, they may be less forgiving for future appointment or deadline blunders.

The Inflexibles

While procrastinators may abound in office environments, there is another type of person and behavior that is less than desirable. These are the inflexibles. As the name denotes, these are individuals who freak out at the sign of any changes to their schedule. If this sounds a tad familiar, it's time for some tough love: Get over it! You are not that important in the corporate scheme of things. Change happens all the time, and it has nothing to do with you.

The key to success in any company is your ability to bend and flex with change. Change will likely impact your life, schedule, goals, milestones, deadlines, and task list. Change may not always be fun and can take you by surprise. You only live once. An adrenaline rush every now and then can keep you on your toes. Too much change, however, can be overbearing and lead to burnout. Understanding how you react and manage change will help you become more adept at change.

As you think about your adaptability to the minor and major changes that have occurred in your personal and professional life, think about the following:

- ▶ What was your typical reaction? Defensive, angry, excited, or optimistic?
- ▶ Are there certain types of changes that cause you to react?
- ▶ What reactions would have been more useful?
- ▶ Given the themes you are noticing, what do you want to commit to doing differently in your new job?
- ▶ How will you remind yourself to keep your reactions productive in upcoming situations?

Your ability to manage your reaction to change will go a long way to helping you become successful in your job. When you can effectively anticipate, manage, and evolve with change, you are better prepared to move in the right company direction and be a leader.

Plan for Disruptions

Distraction is everywhere; it is up to you to be discriminating about what, when, and how you divert your focus from your well-planned schedule. It may be very hard to avoid piqued curiosity and further inquiry when you hear that the vice president of manufacturing had an unfortunate run-in with a mountain lion. However, you may need to exert some self-discipline if you are distracted by the need to play fantasy football and keep up with your friend on Instant Messaging.

It takes discipline to stay focused on the task at hand with so much going on and so many potential diversions.

Aside from the traditional social, biological, and technical distractions, you will find that unforeseen work issues may divert your focus. The effective time manager can quickly adapt. First, validate that what has come before you is truly a priority concern. Second, identify a course of action. No matter what the priority of the surprise, communicate how you will respond to applicable parties. Clue: High-priority surprise equals your manager needs you to review and update an important report before 9:00 A.M. the next day.

Plan for disruptions and interruptions. Sound counterintuitive? It is counterintuitive. How can you plan for something that hasn't happened? Given human nature and the way work gets completed, it is not a surprise that you and your coworker will encounter the following: people who procrastinate, forget things because they are not organized with a task list, or have the horrible luck of unforeseeable tragedies in their life. These issues will not affect you because you have planned for these distractions by making sure you have ample time to do your work. You have strategically created slack in your schedule so that when a surprise enters your world you can make accommodations.

 ## Knowledge

Get out your drill bit and straw, it's time to suck out some juicy bits of knowledge from your coworkers. But before you start gathering your knowledge bits, you will want to understand some of the social dynamics of asking people for their knowledge. Sharing information is like sharing anything of value. Some people may not want to share what they have without knowing what is going to be done with what they give. Imagine giving up the secrets that help you do your job better than anybody else? Surprising, but that is what many people feel they are doing when asked to share their expertise. In order to effectively gather the information you need, you must first be sensitive to others' perceptions and establish trust.

Make the Exchange

It took several attempts to get on a colleague's calendar. You finally found an open slot. Now what? What will you discuss? What can you offer her in return for her time and insights?

Knowledge sharing is an interesting social phenomenon of give and take. As you engage with people, they must feel as though they are getting back as much as they give. What you give in exchange for what you receive depends on the context of the conversation and working relationship. Simply being appreciative of what the person is providing can be enough. You are the judge, and at the very minimum, can volunteer your help if there is anything you can do to assist them in the future.

Additional tips for the exchange include:

▶ Be grateful and never arrogant; they are doing you a favor.
▶ Give credit; cite them as a source.
▶ Let your manager or coworkers know they helped you out.

Get the Bonus Prize

No matter how fertile or reserved a person turns out to be as a knowledge resource, the important thing is that you are having the conversation. Do not walk away empty-handed. Always make sure you ask for suggestions about where you can find additional resources. People do not automatically think to tell you there is a great article on the topic or that Bill down the hall attempted a similar project four years ago. Unless you ask, you may not get it.

You may recognize this technique as the used-car-salesman approach. While it looks cheesy when someone is selling you something that really is a lemon, in your professional life, it pays to not take "no" for an answer. Make three attempts to ask in different ways: who else would be useful for you to talk to, where else can you find additional information, and what else would be helpful for you to know?

 Team

Occasionally we break from the usual workplace optimism to provide a bit of candid advice. As professionals who have balanced the importance of team effectiveness with anger management, we offer the following: Consider the development of your social skills a strategic competency. The better your social skills, the more successful you will be. Because like it or not, your team is now part of your work life. The better you are able to work with it and make a great impression, the easier your work life will be. Open your mind, remove any chips from your shoulder, and smile. At times there may be bitter pills to swallow. As you smile and take a gulp, remember that your coworkers will more than likely be providing input to your boss on your annual performance review. The ball is in your court.

As you have conversations with teammates and coworkers this week, focus on your team skills. Every interaction is an opportunity to demonstrate that you are the embodiment of the team-player philosophy, even if you are a closet introvert who would like nothing more than to be in the peace and solitude of the isolation tank called your office.

Make the First Move

As you gather valuable information, give back to your teammates in the spirit of collaboration. "But what do I have to give?" you ask. "I'm the new guy." Plenty! You must know something about something, right? What about what you've learned through your conversations in the last three weeks? Barring confidential information, there are certainly valuable observations about your new environment that you can share with your team. In addition, you've got professional experience and an interesting background. Remember, they hired you for your experience, observations, and ability to give back to the company through collaborative efforts.

As you focus on being a team player and further developing your collaboration skills, take the initiative to share. Don't wait for someone to ask. To encourage the collaborative behavior of sharing, you must start it yourself.

Show Your Cards

Quickly building relationships with your teammates and coworkers requires that you establish trust. In order to create trust with others, you must show them a part of who you are and provide them insight into your values. But hold on; stop before you go and divulge to your coworkers the most intimate of information. We are not suggesting that you divulge childhood trauma and the one time in the third grade the class bully, Mathilda, took your lunch money—too much information.

To build trust, provide insight into your character and values through your background. This might include information about where you grew up, how large a family you have, or the importance you place on making a contribution to the team. Share information that provides a glimmer into who you are and what you stand for.

"What if they don't want to know?" Good question. Some of your coworkers may not respond well to the bonding opportunity you are offering. Each person and relationship is different. Some folks will want and need to make small talk about your prior experience, where you live, and so forth. Others will want to stick to business. Start by testing the waters. There will be opportunities to build trust and relationships with all types, from those who value personal relationships to those who keep it professional.

Lions, Tigers, and Bears, Oh My!

Hopefully all of your coworkers are kindhearted and only have the best intentions. However, not everyone in your new workplace may be ready to extend a helping hand. If you think you are swimming in shark-infested waters, there are things you can do to validate your opinion and, if necessary, avoid getting bitten. First, don't jump to the conclusion that coworkers are predators. Err on the side of optimism and openness. By keeping an open mind and sharing information, you create an opening to have a conversation with your coworkers to better understand their intent.

There are different types of predators to be aware of, from the common bully to the rare, yet occasionally deadly, smile-to-your-face backstabber. Depending on the type of shark, you have a few options: keep them close, ignore them, or simply tolerate them. When you keep your predators close, show your cards, come from a place of curiosity, and ask questions to understand their concerns. If they do not open up after several attempts, then you may have to move to the next option: ignore the person. If you are in a situation where ignoring your predator is not an option, take the high road and continue to be professional and look for ways to build the relationship.

Sharing Resources

In your conversations, the way you present information is important. Don't offer random resources for the sake of trying to make a contribution. Give it some thought. This information needs to have relevance to be perceived as having value. After you make your offering, see how your teammates respond. Do they ask questions and show interest? You want this to be a two-way conversation. If you offer something up and the response is "That's nice," don't be discouraged. The educated attempt is always worth a try.

At the end of the conversation, ask explicitly if this information was helpful. You want to open yourself up for feedback. It's the best way to understand what resources would be helpful. This allows people to know that you are willing to share information and listen to what others need. Here are some guidelines for sharing what you know.

1. *Be timely*—The information must be timely. If you share it two weeks after the fact, the relevance and value of what you are providing may have diminished.

2. *Be relevant*—The information must be relevant to others and what they are currently working on.

3. *Get permission*—You want to ask the person for permission to share. They may be in the middle of something else, and the timing not good. Give your teammates the opportunity to say yes or no. They will be much more open to receiving information from you when they have a choice.

4. *Choose the venue*—How you share the information is important. In-person meeting, phone call, or e-mail? Depending on the type of information you have to share, you will want to consider the most appropriate method.

5. *Honor confidentiality*—Don't share information that breaches the confidentiality of your coworkers or company. If you have to share confidential information as part of your job, make sure you state that what you are sharing is confidential and should not be shared with others. If you are the recipient of information that you think may be confidential, confirm whether or not it can be shared with others.

 **Image**

During a game of poker, the players pay careful attention to what's going on, observing even the slightest facial expressions, the conversation, and even the silence. The calculating card player realizes that what is being communicated is as important as the cards that each player holds. Your company and the people that work in it are no different. They may not comment to you directly about the behavior they observe. But they do notice, and it does affect how you are perceived. This may sound paranoid, but it's true! Our instincts are directed to constantly take in information from the world around us. We integrate most of our observations into how we make decisions.

Think about what you observe during various interactions with coworkers. Don't you notice when you talk to a coworker who always looks distracted and never seems to make eye contact? It's as if she's constantly preoccupied. Maybe it's the caffeine? Maybe it's problems at home? Whatever it is, it seems like she is in another place. It probably doesn't occur to her that she appears this way. However, as a result of your interactions, you keep your conversations with this individual brief and to the point.

Building the image you want requires being aware of the subtle yin and yang of what you say and how you say it. To help you continue to build your ninja-like image skills, consider the concepts of behavioral and relationship rapport. These are additional skills that will help you communicate and more effectively build trust with teammates and coworkers.

Relationship Rapport

The objective of relationship rapport is to create a connection with the person you are talking with in order to build familiarity, trust, and credibility. This is done through asking questions about interests, background, and potentially similar experiences.

For instance, when you make small talk to find out more about a coworker, you realize that you both went to the same college but in different years. Suddenly you both feel more comfortable. You notice that the other person seems much more relaxed and eager to share information as they walk down nostalgia lane. They ask you if the psychology building still looks like a mental asylum, and you laugh about the silly mascot and that the dreadful school colors have not changed since the turn of the century. Because you have mutual experiences, you have established in the other person a level of credibility and trust.

There will be instances in which you have few to no similarities, and yet you still want to build relationship rapport with your coworker. This is where your curiosity and active listening skills come into play. You build rapport by taking the time to learn more about the other person.

How do you establish relationship rapport? Start with chitchat. "But I hate chitchat," you respond. "It's such a waste of time. I don't want to know about Joan's three kids and what they are each doing in their after-school programs. I don't even have kids myself. I can't relate." It does not matter if you cannot relate. Put on your curious hat and stay with the conversation.

When a coworker shares a personal story, they are revealing information about themselves. Remember the key points of what they are telling you: number of kids, names, and hobbies. The next time you see them and ask how their five-year-old's swim classes are going and if he's mastered his freestyle strokes, odds are you will get a delightful and personable response from the other person because you cared enough to remember. They will feel much more connected to you. You demonstrated that you were interested and listened carefully to their story. You have developed trust.

Your degree of relationship rapport increases with time. Before you know it, you will have strong relationships with coworkers. Your relationships will be strong enough so that when you need a favor or assistance they will be there to help. The great thing about having established rapport and trust is that unless you do something that damages the relationship it will always be there.

Behavioral Rapport

Having common interests is only one aspect of rapport. The second is what is known as behavioral rapport, which is a phrase that comes from the field of neurolinguistic programming (NLP). Don't be intimidated. It has its roots in various disciplines of psychology. No, we are not asking you to be your coworker's therapist.

NLP started in the 1960s in Santa Cruz, California, and is based on the research of Richard Bandler and John Grinder. The findings were quite interesting and applicable to anyone. The pattern that Bandler and Grinder noticed was that when therapists matched their clients' verbal and nonverbal communication patterns they were able to quickly establish trust.

Have you ever had the experience of feeling completely in sync with someone? For some reason, you both naturally mirrored one another. If you videotaped the interaction, you probably would have noticed that your body language looked similar. When you waved your arm with excitement, the other person naturally did the same. You probably even started to sound like the other person. You used the same key words. They said, "No way!" You responded, "Yes way," even though that's not something you would normally say.

You were probably both talking faster and louder because you were having such a great time. That was a fun conversation! Yes, you were in behavioral rapport. This happens naturally when two people are in sync, whether they have known each other for a long time or just met.

If you were to ask the other person later why they felt comfortable, they might tell you that you made good eye contact, listened, and asked questions. While you were doing all these things as part of your active listening skills, you were also demonstrating in your behavior that you are similar to them and therefore not a threat.

Behavioral rapport is a great skill set to add to your active listening skills.

What are the implications for you in the workplace? Well, you could take the chance and hope that you are in sync with the other person. We cannot predict the odds of that. You could increase the likelihood that you are in sync by purposely mirroring the other person—we don't mean mimic them. An exact image is too contrived. General similarities are good enough. Most people will not even notice that you are doing this. For the few who have been trained in this area, most won't notice. As far as they are concerned, the conversation just feels good. Finally, for the even smaller percentages who do notice, they are usually delighted to see you make the effort.

Behavioral Rapport in Action

The critical times to employ behavioral rapport are at the beginning of the conversation to create a sense of familiarity and comfort and during the conversation if differences in opinion arise. In both cases, your intent for matching is to first create comfort/trust and then engage or reengage the person in the conversation as needed.

For example, when someone is upset, most people try to calm them down by demonstrating the exact opposite behavior. Specifically, a person who is upset may point their finger, have furrowed brows, raise their voice, and use harsh language. When we try to calm them down, we naturally act calm, which is the exact opposite behavior. This is a clear mismatch and the opposite of building behavioral rapport. In fact, the person who is upset will feel misunderstood by the calm person, if not patronized. This tends to upset them even more.

In order to demonstrate that you understand their emotional state, you must match and pace the other person before you proceed.

Based on the preceding example, to build behavioral rapport with someone who is upset, you, too, might raise your voice slightly, use similar body language to get their attention, and say forcefully that you understand they are upset. While this may seem like a lot to do to effectively engage someone, it works and will become easier with practice.

What Behaviors to Match

When you are matching the other person, focus your attention on the following four areas: external behavior (what you see), internal behavior (how the other person is feeling), voice (tone and pace), and language (phrases and specific words).

When you match external behavior, notice the other person's body language. This includes their posture, hand gestures, and facial expressions. Posture is important to match. Some people like to lean forward in the conversation, and others like to lean back in their chair. Make sure you match the other person's posture since this particular behavior conveys a lot of information regarding how they are feeling. If the other person is leaning forward and you are leaning back in your chair, the interpretation could be that they think you are not as interested in the conversation. "But I feel comfortable sitting with my arms crossed and leaning back in my chair." It does not matter what your intent was. It's what the other person perceives to be the truth in their mind. Get out of your comfort zone and try out new postures.

You will notice that some people have a tendency to use more hand gestures. If that is the case, try moving your hands more. At first this may feel uncomfortable, but remember no one knows you are trying this out. They are usually so immersed in themselves and how the conversation is going that they won't notice. The same goes with facial expressions; if you find the other person smiles a lot, you will want to do the same.

Match internal behavior if you need to deeply empathize with the person and are finding it difficult to connect with them. Put yourself in their shoes. What does it mean that they are sad right now? What do you think their internal state of being sad feels like? They might feel down, pessimistic, and distracted. When you can match them at the deeper level of emotion, you can more easily understand what they are experiencing. At that point, you operate from a more informed place when it comes to the decisions you make and how you choose to communicate with this person. You may decide that the conversation needs to be postponed if they are too emotional right now. You may decide to express your empathy and boldly state you understand their concerns. When you match the other person's internal state, you demonstrate that you understand why they feel a certain way.

Match the other person's voice quality. Pay attention to the other person's tone and speed. Think about it in the context of being at the library. When you burst out in a loud conversation with your friend, you are not surprised by the nasty look you get from the librarian who reminds you to use your "library voice." So you adjust accordingly. You lower your voice and talk a little slower. This is no different when you are matching another person to get a rapport with them.

How fast is the other person talking? Compare yourself. Do you need to speed up or slow down? Think about the last time you had a conversation with someone who spoke as slow as molasses. Do you remember that feeling of irritation when you tried to get through the conversation quickly and they just didn't hurry up and finish what they had to say? This is a clear pacing mismatch. Monitor how fast the other person talks so you can adjust your pace to establish and stay in rapport.

Your tone of voice conveys a lot of information. If you roll your eyes and sarcastically say "What a great idea," people will know from your body language and tone that you are not in favor of it. Think about the time someone said "Hi" unenthusiastically. Didn't you know they were not happy to see you? Tone of voice is a huge indicator of someone's internal state. It provides additional clues to identify where the person is emotionally and how to best approach them. You will also need to consider your own voice tone to ensure you are sending the message you intend. Get comfortable with adjusting your tone and speed.

Finally, pay attention to the key words or phrases used in your conversations. The same words can have different meanings for different people. To create behavioral rapport, it is important to use the other person's key words and phrases. Ask for clarification using their exact words. You can easily damage rapport if you make an interpretation that is incorrect. It's safer to stick to exact words. Have you ever had the experience of paraphrasing and when you got it wrong it made the situation even worse because you saw a slight twinge of annoyance on the other person's face? Well, your observation was most likely right. Not only did they feel irritated, but they also got the sense that you didn't get what they were trying to say.

Put It All Together

Be your own champion! Now it is time to put ideas into action. The best way to learn is by doing. Immerse yourself in your projects and work life. Meet with the people that can help. Use your rapport building skills to start building trust with your team and coworkers.

Following is your calendar for the week. Plug in what you need to do in Week 4 to make sure you immerse yourself and make progress on your projects. At the end of the week and before you get ready for a well-deserved weekend, take a couple moments to think back on this week. What went well? What did you learn? What do you want to work on or accomplish next week?

Congratulations on completing your fourth week on the job!

Calendar for Week ④ Day ① 2 3 4 5

Time	Action	Notes
6:00 A.M.		
7:00 A.M.		
8:00 A.M.		
9:00 A.M.		
10:00 A.M.		
11:00 A.M.		
12:00 P.M.		
1:00 P.M.		
2:00 P.M.		
3:00 P.M.		
4:00 P.M.		
5:00 P.M.		
6:00 P.M.		
7:00 P.M.		

REMINDERS

▶ Review your task list for the week.

▶ Get clear on your milestones.

▶ Prepare for your meetings with colleagues to gather information.

Calendar for Week ④ Day 1 ② 3 4 5

Time	Action	Notes
6:00 A.M.		
7:00 A.M.		
8:00 A.M.		
9:00 A.M.		
10:00 A.M.		
11:00 A.M.		
12:00 P.M.		
1:00 P.M.		
2:00 P.M.		
3:00 P.M.		
4:00 P.M.		
5:00 P.M.		
6:00 P.M.		
7:00 P.M.		

REMINDERS

► Practice your relationship rapport-building skills.
► Review how you are managing your time in getting to and from work and making it to your meetings on time.

Calendar for Week ④ Day 1 2 ③ 4 5

Time	Action	Notes
6:00 A.M.		
7:00 A.M.		
8:00 A.M.		
9:00 A.M.		
10:00 A.M.		
11:00 A.M.		
12:00 P.M.		
1:00 P.M.		
2:00 P.M.		
3:00 P.M.		
4:00 P.M.		
5:00 P.M.		
6:00 P.M.		
7:00 P.M.		

REMINDERS

▶ Plan for distractions during the day. What are the distractions that mostly come up?

▶ Pay attention to your project scope and goal. Is it changing or staying the same?

▶ Practice your behavioral-rapport skills, specifically matching body language.

Calendar for Week (4) Day 1 2 3 (4) 5

Time	Action	Notes
6:00 A.M.		
7:00 A.M.		
8:00 A.M.		
9:00 A.M.		
10:00 A.M.		
11:00 A.M.		
12:00 P.M.		
1:00 P.M.		
2:00 P.M.		
3:00 P.M.		
4:00 P.M.		
5:00 P.M.		
6:00 P.M.		
7:00 P.M.		

REMINDERS

▶ Practice your behavioral-rapport skills, specifically match tone of voice.

▶ Make sure your conversations with coworkers feel equitable. What did you give in return for their time and insights?

Calendar for Week ④ Day 1 2 3 4 ⑤

Time	Action	Notes
6:00 A.M.		
7:00 A.M.		
8:00 A.M.		
9:00 A.M.		
10:00 A.M.		
11:00 A.M.		
12:00 P.M.		
1:00 P.M.		
2:00 P.M.		
3:00 P.M.		
4:00 P.M.		
5:00 P.M.		
6:00 P.M.		
7:00 P.M.		

REMINDERS

▶ Practice your behavioral-rapport skills, specifically matching key words.

▶ Plan your tasks for next week.

Chapter 5

WEEK 5   Climb onto the Observation Deck

■■ Last week was good, but it could have been better. At a meeting, people were socializing, and I mentioned that it was ten minutes after the hour. It appears that I tried to get down to business too quickly. In fact, I jumped into the meeting agenda a little too soon. I got a few funny looks and could feel my face getting flushed. I felt pretty embarrassed. This might seem like a trivial thing, but when you're new, you don't want to make mistakes like that.

"I am still getting used to the differences between my old company and this new one. It's amazing how different some things are and how those little things, like spending almost a quarter of the meeting socializing, turn out to be an important part of the culture. In my old job, meetings were much more formal—we had an agenda and specific goals to achieve during the meeting. It was definitely a more serious, get-down-to-business environment. It got me thinking about how people work together and the kinds of things that are important to people in my new company. I guess socializing can be an important part of doing the work. ■■

MONTH 1
● ● ● ● ●
● ● ● ● ●
● ● ● ● ●
● ● ● ● ●

MONTH 2
● ● ● ● ●
○ ○ ○ ○ ○
○ ○ ○ ○ ○
○ ○ ○ ○ ○

MONTH 3
○ ○ ○ ○ ○
○ ○ ○ ○ ○
○ ○ ○ ○ ○
○ ○ ○ ○ ○

You have been surrounded by the wilderness that is your new job. In every job there are both formal and informal ways in which work gets accomplished. The formal stuff is all around you—the rules and regulations pertaining to your conduct—no throwing pencils and running down the halls, deadline structures, arrival times, and other company policies. The formal ways in which work gets done in your company are dictated by its policies and procedures, management styles, and specific products or services. However, as you spend more time in your job, you will probably realize that maybe there's more than meets the eye. There is. That's the informal stuff. It's the juicy part of really learning to successfully navigate through your new company by understanding the unwritten rules and ways that work gets done.

Put on a pair of X-ray company decoder goggles. Be a corporate scientist and peer beneath the surface to look closer at the inner workings of your company. You're going to see a fascinating environment

Week 5 Sink or Swim Skills	Overall Objective: Identify Methods and Processes for How Work Gets Done
Goals	Identify successful ways in which work gets completed.
Time	Observe how time is treated, valued, and managed.
Knowledge	Identify how information is shared.
Team	Observe and understand how your team gets work done, collaborates, and functions.
Image	Observe your environment, how others who are considered successful dress and behave, how you are adapting, and make the necessary adjustments.

full of rituals, unwritten rules, and practices. Observe familiar creatures such as Homo coworkerectus in a subtle new light, document your discoveries, and apply your observations to your job. When you decode your work environment, you will be amazed at how much better you will be able to navigate around potential obstacles and achieve your objectives. Now put on your goggles. It's time for adventure!

 Goals

In many of the organizations we've worked with, we have been amazed to see the allocation of lots of money toward projects without first clearly defining a project goal. This might be easily brushed off as a curious and quirky trait except for the fact that more often than not projects without clear goals become a waste of time and money. How your company and coworkers establish and accomplish goals should be very important to you. As the newbie, ensure that you can accomplish what you set out to achieve. Also when the opportunity arises, the importance you place on clarifying the goals will allow you to be the voice of reason and help positively influence your team and company. Direct your spirit of inquiry to the following items.

Decisions, Decisions . . .

A fundamental component of getting work done is making decisions. Decisions get made based on leadership influence, cultural elements such as the importance of collaboration, or the type of work that gets done. There's a range of decision-making possibilities from the quick-and-easy-leader-provided "yes" or "no" to the more inclusive, slower-moving consensus approach.

Observe how decisions get made in your company. Is your company big on collaboration? If so, in order to get decisions made regarding your work, you may need to include a number of people to get their support. Are decisions usually made by a few key decision-makers (i.e., your manager)? If this is the case, you will want to know how to best communicate your ideas. Another important part of decision-making is determining what influences people's decisions. Some people need lots of facts and figures while others make decisions based on relationships. When you understand how decisions get made, you will know how to gain the support of others for a decision to be made in your favor.

Priorities

The importance of a goal should correlate directly with the priorities of your team and company. A common problem is not limiting the priorities to the critical few. The result is a list of ten or fifteen top priorities, which is ridiculous. When everything is a top priority, no one knows what to do first. Organizations, teams, and individuals should have no more than three top priorities at any time. As work piles on your plate, it will be critical to understand how work is prioritized in order for you to focus your efforts in the right direction.

Company leadership, customer demands, and unexpected events can each play an influential part in setting priorities. If you need clarification on your company's and team's top priorities, talk with your manager. Ask how these priorities were established. In addition, take a look at your current projects to see how they fit with the identified priorities. Sometimes the way things are prioritized is different than how you would do it. Do your best to set realistic expectations for what you can accomplish, and go with the flow.

Selling Your Big Ideas

So you have an idea for how you can save the company money. Who do you go to in order to get support for your idea? Find out the protocol for getting new ideas started. This may be as simple as sharing the idea with your manager or as complex as researching and developing a formal proposal. In addition, tap into your network to determine who else you may want (or need) as part of your plan.

Everybody Can Use a Hand Sometimes

We all need help whether it's in the form of a budget, information, or an extra set of hands. But successfully getting the help you need may take some insight. Make some observations. When and how do people make requests for help? What is the basis for getting this help? Is it based on who is willing to open their mouth and ask or only based on strict budget guidelines? What resources are available? Once again, success is all about understanding the underlying protocol and steps for successfully getting assistance to accomplish your goals.

Play Nicely Together

Unless you work the winter shift at a forest-fire observation station, your job probably involves some level of collaboration with people, teams, and departments. You have had an opportunity to witness how well collaboration takes place. Think about your experiences. Do people talk about the value of working together but work on their own? Does partnering with a coworker require a certain amount of trust or an existing relationship? Do teams and organizations share information or partner on projects? Another aspect of collaboration is defining how working together and sharing takes place. Identify various methods, technology, or protocol and integrate this into how you work with others.

 Time

Are you feeling like a road runner among penguins, or are you in sync with the pace of your new company? As you probably have noticed, your new company has a distinct way of valuing time. It is very important that you are aware of the pace of your work environment, how time is treated in your company, and how you compare. The last thing you want is the company nickname "turtle," nor do you want to be considered the quad-shot, nonfat, mochaccino speed freak. In order to get an idea of how you are fitting in to your company from a time perspective, you will need to understand your company's time-related values.

Importance of Time

Understanding the value that is placed on deadlines, schedules, and differentiating between what people say they want and what actually happens will help you to plan, prioritize, and successfully navigate through the logistical irregularities in your company.

Time is treated very differently by each organization. You may find that meetings are set to begin at the top of the hour. Yet, everyone knows that if they arrive on time they will be sitting alone for a good five minutes. So everyone purposely shows up at the meeting five minutes late. The same goes for behaviors related to deadlines. Are they steadfast or flexible? What are the effects of this? In general, what you do notice about how coworkers meet deadlines and respond to e-mail and phone messages? Do people respond promptly?

Be aware of these practices since they will help you effectively follow rules and guidelines. They will also provide you with the opportunity to influence and role model more professional behaviors such as starting meetings on time, meeting deadlines, and responding promptly (within twenty-four hours) to incoming e-mail and voice mail.

Roaring Rapids or Sunday Cruise—Find the Pace

Look around; do people in your company scurry like hamsters on espresso or move at a glacier's pace? Is the pace in my company intense or laid back? What about your company makes it this way? For instance, is work that was requested of you today expected to be done yesterday, or do people start feeding you ideas early on and let the ideas bake for a couple of weeks before making any commitments? Keep in mind the pace of your new company. Adjust your own speed up a notch or two to be more in sync. Conversely, you may want to cool your jets a little bit if you find yourself leaving your coworkers in the dust. You are the judge and it's important that you understand the pace so as to stay in sync with everyone else.

Time and the Bigger Picture

Take a look at your company's strategy. Is it focused on long-, short-, or medium-term objectives? Look at how it is planning on reaching these objectives. Some companies focus on a short-term, fast-growth strategy while others focus on slower, long-term steady growth. Time at an organization level is significantly influenced by the type of industry. For example, it may take a drug company ten years to get a product to market while it takes a software company two years to develop a new version. However, no matter what the industry, it is important to understand the correlation of time to current strategy, planning, and broader organization objectives. If your company is completely focused on the immediate pressures of today, it may be missing a number of opportunities that will require long-range planning.

Many companies know that to be effective it takes a combination of balancing the urgency of short-term objectives with planting the seeds for long-term success. But like people, there is a tendency for companies to focus on one element more than another. You may find that your company says it is important to focus on the future; yet they spend very little money on research and development and only focus on putting all of their efforts and dollars toward hiring sales people to make the sales numbers for this quarter. Understanding this larger perspective will help you have a better understanding of why decisions get made a certain way.

 Knowledge

Although you may not realize it, you are a knowledge worker. A "knowledge worker" is the kind of employee whose most important resources are in their head—not their hands. This is a tremendous workplace evolutionary shift from the idea that your worth is based on physical stamina and speed to the idea of your worth as based on education, mental skills, and acumen. In your new company, the most valuable resource is the knowledge of its employees.

Knowledge, where you find it and how it is shared, is equally important in how you will succeed in your new job.

E-mails, Meetings, and Intranet

Identify the standard procedures for sharing information. Look for the ways information is shared such as e-mail and meetings. What are people's preferences? Also look at how information is shared at different levels and groups in the organization. Do company senior leaders use different methods than midlevel management to share information? Be aware of specific protocols and practices. Are only certain types of information shared in meetings, while other types are shared in e-mail? Depending on your company, information may be treated as a protected resource or freely shared. Also, as you share what you know, predefine your audience, appropriate method of sharing, and whether or not the information is appropriate to the audience.

The Insiders

In every company, there are people who are "in the know." They have the inside scoop on what is really happening. It's the kind of information that impacts your day-to-day activities, but no one tells you in a memo or during a team meeting. These informal sources of information can be critical resources to get the insider's view of the company and how things really get done. Access to the information is based on relationships and trust. Who are the people you work with who always seem to be in the know? Don't stress if you have not identified or made a trusted relationship with an insider. Building these relationships may take time.

Also, be cautious that as a new person some people will offer you the supposed "inside" information or "real deal." Take all company gossip with a grain of salt. The sad fact is that while you'd like to think every coworker is out to help you, some may try to misguide you, have their own agenda, or be misguided themselves. You definitely do not want to get tagged in your first few weeks as a troublemaker or someone who is gullible enough to become the effect of someone else's bad information. Start slowly; focus on building relationships first. The insider information will follow.

Sorry, We Don't Do That Here

Most living organisms have three primary responses upon being exposed to new things: fight, flight, or acceptance. When introducing new ideas, companies are pretty much the same way. They can eagerly accept a new idea, push back and reject the idea, or try to ignore it and hope it goes away. In order to ensure that your ideas are accepted, be aware of how new ideas are treated and what you can do to gain maximum acceptance. It takes some people time to get used to an idea. It has to grow on them. Others may be initially resistant to new ideas and information because they impact their own projects or agendas. Notice how much information or time people need in order to adopt or try something new.

Check Your Sources

An important aspect of knowledge or information is ensuring that the source of the information is respected in your company. Quoting *Reader's Digest* may work for some companies, but others may hold other sources in higher regard. In some companies, academic and scientific data is the standard, while in other companies, field experience is more important. What's the case in your company? As you understand what kind of information is deemed credible, it will help you identify and gather the appropriate kind of information to share with others and support your ideas and plans.

Learning Organization or Reinvention

A big part of managing knowledge is making sure that what is learned from various projects is shared with the rest of the company. Part of understanding your real work environment requires defining if, when, and how knowledge from projects is shared so you are not reinventing the wheel. Is there a process for learning from earlier endeavors? Do people hold onto the information without even thinking of how they can share?

A postmortem is a process by which after projects and goals are accomplished, the company, department, or team reviews what was learned (i.e., mistakes and successes) and what can be passed on to the rest of the company. This reduces redundancies, inefficiencies, and possibly prevents costly future mistakes. Although this may sound intuitive and obvious to you, you'd be surprised how many companies do not keep track of their knowledge and lessons learned.

Show Me the Money

As much as leaders in a company say they value and support sharing knowledge, there might be very little sharing that goes on unless there are rewards or consequences for not sharing. Look around. Are people rewarded for sharing? Are there consequences for not sharing? Is sharing knowledge and resources practiced by leaders in your company? This will help you identify how to gather the resources you need, as well as understand how to successfully share what you have with others.

For example, if sharing knowledge is not a common practice in your new company, you will have to take more time to explain why you are looking for information, what you plan on doing with it, and make sure that you acknowledge the other person's contribution.

 **Team**

Sometimes you might feel like your new company is more like a mental institution than a business. You are not alone. The biggest challenge to a new employee in any company is to understand the various dynamics of how people work together. In order to be successful, you have to understand both the individual personas of your coworkers and also some of the more potentially taboo topics such as company politics, nepotism, or turf guarding. The sooner you understand various company personality traits, the more effective you will be at navigating any potential floating mines—and you'll continue to thrive. The need to understand these subtle traits is even more important with your team. Here are some areas to keep in mind.

It's What Makes Your Team Unique

Each team has a distinct personality. As you spend time with your team, you have probably observed specific traits or characteristics.

Once again, we are talking about the more subtle traits that may not have been initially obvious, such as underlying team dynamics, what is important to the team, and how work gets accomplished. Some teams may be much more competitive and emphasize doing better than other teams. Other teams may focus on the importance and value of relationships and team building.

Understand the unique elements of your team to help you determine where to apply your efforts. Some questions to consider include: Do teammates share equally with every member or only with specific individuals? What are the personality dynamics among your teammates? Do certain people have more or less influence, and why? You may notice that certain individuals have areas of expertise or communication skills that may help their ability to influence others.

Think about the kinds of things people listen to and consider important.

Values? What Values?

Most organizations have spent time and money identifying a set of corporate values. Sometimes these values become an integrated part of the way the company conducts business. At other times, the list of corporate values becomes nothing more than a neglected poster tucked away in a desk drawer. Does your team have a set of values that it follows? Understand your team's values whether they are written down or implied. Observe if your team's behaviors are consistent with these values. Remember, although you may be new, you still influence your team. Make sure your behaviors are consistent with the team values, despite the behaviors of your teammates. You have an opportunity to be a role model.

We Say It and We Mean It

"I will send you that information later." Possible translations: "You will have that information in the next hour" or "You will have that information whenever I remember to send it your way." Depending on the person or the company, that sentence can mean a number of different things.

Digging a bit deeper into the specifics of team behavior, it is important to understand how teammates and other coworkers make and follow through on commitments. You build credibility through defining and following through on expectations. Notice how your team follows through on commitments that are made. Do people provide you the information in the time you requested? Do people meet deadlines and keep to schedules?

Blame Game or Accountability

Observe how the people on your team hold themselves accountable. Whether or not they keep commitments is one thing. But when they are unable to keep their commitments, do they take every action necessary to keep you informed and updated? Do they point the finger at others and say it's not their fault? The sign of a strong team is commitment, communication, and accountability.

Turf Guarding

Although this may sound less like corporate America and more like an urban gang issue, turf guarding is common in most companies. As the new person, you might have already encountered it.

How can you recognize it? Turf-guarding symptoms may include apprehension to share information, individuals or groups that tightly control valuable resources, and managers that refuse to collaborate with other groups. Hopefully, your teammates and others do want to truly collaborate and do not guard their turf or territory. You may find that there are people on your team who are concerned that if two of you partner on a project, you will get all the credit and look good and they will look bad.

There is a reason why people guard their territory. It is typically out of fear of losing resources, control, or credibility. It is a natural reaction, albeit counterproductive. If you find yourself in this situation with a colleague, find out what their concerns are about and navigate carefully. Alleviate coworker concerns through careful stroking of ego and well-placed compliments. Give credit to your teammates in front of your manager. If you come up against intense turf guarding and you cannot get the resources you need to do your job, you may need to call in air support and involve a member of the management team to resolve the issue and clarify specific roles and responsibilities.

 **Image**

So you think you are the image of dressing for success with a look that says 100 percent business? Little do you know that your coworkers in the logistics department, who wear jeans five days a week, call you the stockbroker when you're not around. You might be working hard and doing a good job, but if you aren't looking around to identify what is considered successful in terms of dress, behavior, and overall image, you might be missing a big blind spot. To ensure that you are not walking around with a sign that says "clueless" taped to the back of your shirt, take stock of your image-management program.

Dressing the Part or Missing the Boat

How are the leaders in the company dressed? How are your coworkers dressed? How do you compare? It's important to take a look at all three categories as you compare and contrast. You may want to fit in with your coworkers, but if your goal is to be a leader in the company, kick it up a notch while still fitting in. Use sound judgment. Keep the Hawaiian shirts for the company barbecue. Pay attention to all of these seemingly subtle elements. When effectively applied, each little detail adds up to present an image of strength and success.

What Gets Listened To

Take a few seconds to consider all the things that you hear each day. What are the characteristics of what you hear that you hold on to because you think it is important? How much of what you say do you think stands out in people's minds? As part of crafting your image, pay attention to what gets heard and remembered. A good place to begin is by observing how successful people in the company communicate. What makes them effective when they have conversations? Do you find that they are polite, do not interrupt, and ask lots of good questions? What kind of statements do they make? Do they support what they say with facts or references?

Defining That Certain Something

What do you notice are the characteristics of effective leaders in the company? What do these individuals seem to know, what are the skills they seem to have, and what are the behaviors they seem to exhibit? You may find that the effective people in the company are not the ones who know everything and can regurgitate a software programming language off the top of their head. Effective leaders are able to apply what they know, see the big picture, take the initiative to communicate their ideas, and inspire others. How do you compare? Do you have the knowledge, skills, and behaviors that seem to be valued in your company? What opportunities are there for development?

Put It All Together

Be your own champion! Now it is time to put ideas into action. As you work this week, remember to keep your eyes and ears open. As any good scientist would do, take notes and give yourself some time to reflect on the observations that you make. Most importantly, begin to define how your observations will affect how you get work done, communicate with coworkers, or do things differently. Confirm your observations and thoughts with a trusted coworker or two.

Following is your calendar for the week. Plug in what you need to do in Week 5 to make sure you begin to explore, define, and decipher your real work environment. At the end of the week and before you get ready for a well-deserved weekend, take a couple moments to think back on this week. What went well? What did you learn? What do you want to work on or accomplish next week?

Congratulations on completing your fifth week on the job!

Calendar for Week (5) Day (1) 2 3 4 5

Time	Action	Notes
6:00 A.M.		
7:00 A.M.		
8:00 A.M.		
9:00 A.M.		
10:00 A.M.		
11:00 A.M.		
12:00 P.M.		
1:00 P.M.		
2:00 P.M.		
3:00 P.M.		
4:00 P.M.		
5:00 P.M.		
6:00 P.M.		
7:00 P.M.		

REMINDERS

▶ Determine my company's and team's values. How are they a part of my day-to-day work?

▶ Is my style of dress sending the right message?

Calendar for Week (5) Day 1 (2) 3 4 5

Time	Action	Notes
6:00 A.M.		
7:00 A.M.		
8:00 A.M.		
9:00 A.M.		
10:00 A.M.		
11:00 A.M.		
12:00 P.M.		
1:00 P.M.		
2:00 P.M.		
3:00 P.M.		
4:00 P.M.		
5:00 P.M.		
6:00 P.M.		
7:00 P.M.		

REMINDERS

► Find out how people take accountability for their actions.
► Identify the traits and characteristics that make my team or coworkers unique.

Calendar for **Week** (**5**) **Day** 1 2 (**3**) 4 5

Time	Action	Notes
6:00 A.M.		
7:00 A.M.		
8:00 A.M.		
9:00 A.M.		
10:00 A.M.		
11:00 A.M.		
12:00 P.M.		
1:00 P.M.		
2:00 P.M.		
3:00 P.M.		
4:00 P.M.		
5:00 P.M.		
6:00 P.M.		
7:00 P.M.		

REMINDERS

▶ Identify how decisions get made.
▶ Determine the values my coworkers consider important.

Calendar for Week ⑤ Day 1 2 3 ④ 5

Time	Action	Notes
6:00 A.M.		
7:00 A.M.		
8:00 A.M.		
9:00 A.M.		
10:00 A.M.		
11:00 A.M.		
12:00 P.M.		
1:00 P.M.		
2:00 P.M.		
3:00 P.M.		
4:00 P.M.		
5:00 P.M.		
6:00 P.M.		
7:00 P.M.		

REMINDERS

► Determine how people share information or knowledge.

► Identify the sources of information that are considered credible.

Calendar for Week ⑤ Day 1 2 3 4 ⑤

Time	Action	Notes
6:00 A.M.		
7:00 A.M.		
8:00 A.M.		
9:00 A.M.		
10:00 A.M.		
11:00 A.M.		
12:00 P.M.		
1:00 P.M.		
2:00 P.M.		
3:00 P.M.		
4:00 P.M.		
5:00 P.M.		
6:00 P.M.		
7:00 P.M.		

REMINDERS

► Consider how teammates follow through on commitments.

► Plan your tasks for next week.

Chapter 6

WEEK 6 **Ignite Your Star Power**

▮▮Wow! Six weeks on the job already. Last week I met with one of the people my manager referred me to in marketing. I was really impressed with this guy. He was clearly an expert in his area, and everyone in the company knows to go to him for his advice. It got me thinking . . . I know a little about a lot of things and a lot about a few things. I wonder what people think of me and what I'm good at doing. More importantly, what do I want to be known for in the company?▮▮

MONTH 1

• • • • •
• • • • •
• • • • •
• • • • •

MONTH 2

• • • • •
• • • • •
• • • • •
• • • • •

MONTH 3

• • • • •
• • • • •
• • • • •
• • • • •

Up to this point, you have been observing, applying, and working on developing your skills. In week six, focus on the unique skills, knowledge, and abilities that you bring to your job. Identify what distinguishes you. Defining what makes you unique will enable you to better utilize your skills, share more effectively with your team and others in your organization, and identify opportunities for further professional development. This will also help you to zero in on the specific skills, traits, or other abilities that you want to be known for.

Goals

In the last five weeks, you have looked at developing your sink or swim skills and making yourself a valuable employee. This week you will take stock of what you have accomplished and focus on your individual strengths and how to highlight them during your work.

Before you can float to the top, identify what makes you unique. How does this goal help you achieve success in your job and overall career? The answer is simple. When you identify what makes you unique relative to others in your environment, it provides you with the ability to differentiate your specific strengths from theirs. Having this awareness allows you to know when and where to effectively apply your skills, clearly communicate what you have to offer coworkers so they understand your abilities, and identify opportunities for further development. In addition, identifying what makes

Week 6 *Sink or Swim* Skills	Overall Objective: Reflect and Identify What Makes You Distinct
Goals	Determine your unique skills and attributes.
Time	Make the time to reflect and gain perspective on what makes you unique and what you are learning in your new job.
Knowledge	Identify what you know, determine subject areas, and determine how to apply your knowledge to your job.
Team	Get feedback on your performance and share your thoughts/reflections/ideas.
Image	Work on developing and delivering your personal PR message.

you unique helps direct your focus to more successfully create a path for your career at your company.

I Am Special

Yes, your mother was right; you are special and not just because you have ear lobes the size of dinner plates. You mean there really is truth to what she was saying all these years? Of course! But like anything else in life, you must believe it in order for it to be true. Once you believe that it's true, you will act in accordance with that notion. Therefore, it is important for your success that you get over whether or not you are special and just accept that you are.

In the context of your career, the skills that make you unique may fall in a variety of areas. In many cases, what makes a person unique is not related to their business, trade, or profession but to inherent personality traits. For example, what may make a doctor shine at their profession is not only the ability to prescribe the right medication, but, more importantly, their natural ability to ask the right questions to better understand a patient's state.

As you begin to consider what makes you unique, think about the skills or traits that come naturally to you. The rest of the chapter outlines how to think about this and, more specifically, how to discover and utilize this information.

As you've learned so far from your practice in setting goals, we are asking that you set a goal to determine what makes you distinct and special. Complete this activity within the next couple of weeks, because you will use the information in the near future. Don't forget your goal-setting skills: identify the milestones, resources, and additional sources for more information. What will success look like? How will you know that you have completed this objective?

unique. Defining what you know is critical to making the most of your abilities. Most of us take for granted the gold mine of information that resides in our heads. It's easy not to be aware of what you know because you generally use it on a daily basis without really considering whether it is unique and worthy of sharing with others. It's time to take a look under the lid and see what's cooking in that great big brain of yours. Start by reviewing the following questions:

- ▶ What am I good at?
- ▶ What are skills I have?
- ▶ What do I know (education, training, experience)?
- ▶ When and why do people come to me for information?
- ▶ What makes my perspective unique from others?
- ▶ What personality traits differentiate me from others?

These are questions that will take time to answer. Ask yourself these questions and let them marinate for a while. Some answers may come quickly; others will take more time. The culmination of what you know is a blend of your skills, experience, perspectives, and personality traits.

Once you identify some conclusions and further insight into what you know, identify specific ways to apply this to your job. For instance, you may find in your reflection that people usually come to you for your personal observations of a situation (i.e., sanity check) and not necessarily for the facts. Your unique qualities are your ability to pay attention to your environment and pick up on the nuances that others miss. To leverage your strength, you may want to more actively contribute your observations, instead of waiting for people to come and ask you.

With the Flow or Swimming Upstream

Being new, there is a delicate balance between making effective contributions and shaking things up too much. As you consider your strengths and what you want to contribute, be aware of the most effective ways to make your suggestions heard and utilized. Specifically, what kind of input can the team and company actually digest?

There may be times when your ideas or recommendations are too new or too big a change for the team to immediately warm up to. How is that possible? Isn't that what the company hired you to do . . . put forth your best ideas? Although the company is paying you to contribute and add value, there will be times when the company is not ready to hear what you have to say . . . even though that's the reason they hired you.

There are some companies that can handle revolutionary changes and reinvent themselves overnight, and there are companies for whom change is evolutionary and incremental. Pay attention to this as you contribute your star power to the team and company. Determine how much they can and will be able to handle at a time. Start slowly and test the waters. If people's reactions are strong, step back a little and observe more. If people like your ideas and suggestions, see how far they will actually run with them before you offer up another one.

 **Team**

As you light the fuse and ignite your star power, you want to ensure that you are heading in the right direction. The last thing you want is to go zooming off in one direction, only to realize you may need to do a U-turn. An excellent way to ensure that you are on the right track is to gather feedback about how you are performing and compare what you think you are doing well with how others perceive you.

While it is important that you think through and even check out some of your assumptions with a trusted friend or significant other, there are other sources from which to gather additional information and check out your assumptions . . . your manager and team.

Feedback from Your Manager

Feedback. Don't be afraid of the word. It's gotten a bad rap because most people do not give feedback very well. Despite this issue, getting others' input on specific components of your behavior or performance can be critical to fine-tuning your development. While the importance of gathering feedback may be common sense, few do it because of apprehension or not knowing how to ask.

It is very important that you gather feedback during the first weeks on the job. Imagine your horror to learn after six months on the job that you are actually not performing up to others' expectations. It's always easier to seek feedback than to have someone tell you out of the blue that you are not doing well, because then you are psychologically prepared for the news—good or bad.

You may ask, "What if my boss is vague and tells me I'm doing fine?" While that is good information, it does not necessarily help you determine your specific strengths or opportunities for development or allow you to ignite your star power. If you are unclear on what doing "fine" entails, probe a little bit more and ask what exactly he thinks is going well, what skills you contribute to the group, and where you can utilize those skills on other projects down the road. In addition, you might want to ask if there is anything he recommends you do differently. Don't push it if he comes back with an equally vague answer. If you press too much, you may start to look insecure. Ask the question once and see what you get back.

Use the feedback your manager provides to confirm what you do well and identify opportunities for further development. Ask for feedback regularly. You might feel a little funny and a bit vulnerable asking someone to comment on how they think you are doing; after a few times, it will feel like a normal part of your job. Don't be a mushroom and live in darkness and hope that what you think matches up with reality. Confirm your hopes by shining some light on your assumptions through getting feedback.

Feedback from Your Teammates

Your teammates are a great source of information. If there are a few individuals you are comfortable with, find a casual opportunity to ask them for feedback. It is important that you ask casually because you don't want them to think you are insecure or making this a big deal. The next time you happen to catch them in the hallway you could gently ask, "So Mike, you've been on this team longer than I have. Is there anything you notice that I could do differently to be more effective?"

Don't be surprised if the feedback you get is more general, such as "You're doing great." "Everyone seems to like you." "Just make sure you watch out for the project scope changing on you. We've all had that happen to us." This is pretty common when you are new and ask for feedback. People may not feel completely comfortable yet and will tend to give you suggestions about pitfalls to avoid. That's okay. You've gotten some great insights and also confirmed that you are generally doing fine.

If You Really Must Know . . .

The most important thing about asking for feedback from team-mates is to ensure that there isn't something glaring that you are missing and is annoying people to death. Although it might be a challenge after being told how your habit of biting your nails is making the team absolutely crazy and you discover that your team nickname is "the Clipper," it is always important to thank the person for giving you feedback. It's easier for a person to say to you that everything is fine versus actually stopping to think about what you are specifically doing great and what areas you might want to be aware of.

Integrate the information your teammates share with you. If they give you specific information or suggestions, such as how you can do better by coming to meetings more prepared with facts and figures, integrate this to ignite your star power. If they tell you are doing well, keep up the good work.

Recap

Here are some guidelines for effectively asking for and receiving feedback.

- ▶ Be specific when asking for feedback. Identify a specific behavior, event, or project.
- ▶ If you receive a general or vague answer, try to probe deeper, that is, "Will you elaborate what you mean by fine?" If your additional query fails to elicit further comment, let it rest.
- ▶ Always thank the person for their feedback no matter how reassuring or surprising your new bits of information are.

Deadwood or Fire Starter?

Is it enough to collect information from your manager, team, coworkers, and your own self-evaluation about your progress and contribution? Of course not! Getting the information is only the first step. It's time to review and act upon what you have learned.

First, are you noticing a trend in what your boss and teammates are telling you? You want to evaluate what they have all said and compare it to your perceptions so as to develop your own conclusion about your strengths and potential blind spots.

Next, think about how you want to apply this information. For instance, if just about everyone is telling you that you are great at generating spreadsheets and doing the analysis, you want to make sure you involve yourself in projects that clearly utilize your strength. In this example, it would be involving yourself in more projects that allow you to play around with numbers.

Something to also keep in mind is that after a while you may get bored with what it is that you are good at and wish to try something new. Make a mental note of this since you will want to include this in the long-term development plan that you will develop in later weeks. In the meantime, your strength is your star power; find ways to utilize it!

 **Image**

As you get clear on what skills and traits make up your star power and add value to your team and company, it is important that your image be consistent with what you want to be known for. In the User Instructions introduction to this book, we talked about how the show must go on despite your all of the events in your life. Your intentional professional image is based on your personal public relations plan. Why? Like any product, we have a perception of what the product delivers and stands for based on the message that comes across in the marketing campaign. It is equally important that you have your own marketing campaign.

Consciously or not, you are always selling yourself to others, whether it is to pitch your idea to your teammates or to have them think of you when they need help on a cool new project. You want good news about you to spread throughout the company and for your name and face to be synonymous with certain values.

It's time to create your PR message. What do you want to be known for? What do you want the association to be when people think of you? When you think about how to craft and deliver your message, always consider the five *Ws*: *why, what, who, when,* and *where.*

Craft Your Message

Think back to the example in the User Instructions introduction on PR and to the car manufacturer Volvo. These cars are synonymous with safety. They are designed and marketed with that intent. The ad campaigns contain visual depictions of family, safety belts, airbags, and other elements of the vehicle's safety-performance features. In conjunction with these visual depictions, the word associations in the ad campaign are all about safety. Similarly, you want to send a consistent message through what you say and do. You may not have airbags and five-point seat belts, but we are confident that you have other high-performance features.

The intent of your PR message is to communicate your values and what you want to be known for. As you think about your professional legacy and strengths, what are some key words that best capture this information? Find three key words or phrases that represent what you want to be known for. Once you have determined them, deliver this message to others.

Every conversation is an opportunity to deliver your message. Let's say you want to be known for follow-through and accountability. Your conversations may sound like this: "It's important to me that we are accountable to our deadlines. I propose we reprioritize some of these projects and renegotiate the deadlines. What do you think?"

Remember, your actions must be consistent with your words. If you want to be known for being reliable and you say to someone "It's important to me that you can rely on me. I'll get you the document by tomorrow" and you don't, you have undermined your message. Make sure your behavior is aligned with your message.

Finally, in addition to your behavior, make sure your physical appearance is consistent with your message. This includes how you groom and present yourself as well as your body language. As we mentioned in Week 4, when developing behavioral rapport, communication is much more than what comes out of your mouth. Showing up in shorts and flip-flops, arriving late to meetings, and leaning back in your chair with your feet up on the table is not consistent with your value of being a hard worker and doing what it takes to get the job done. Make sure how you show up is consistent with the three key messages you chose.

Deliver Your Message

So far we explained *why* this is important and discussed the *what* or content of your message. We are now left with three *W*s. Let's look at the *who, when,* and *where* of delivering your message. As indicated earlier, e-mails, phone conversations, and face-to-face meetings are all great venues for *where* to deliver your message.

Choose the appropriate venue to deliver your message. After you define and articulate your values in your PR message, use e-mail as your initial method of communication. In that way, you can draft your message, read it, and reread it so that it makes sense and is in your own words. We recommend using the prompt "It is important to me that . . ." This sets up the recipient to take in something of significance to you. You are explicit. After a few practice e-mail drafts, you will be ready to deliver your message in face-to-face and phone conversations.

Next, determine if the timing is right, that is, *when*. Keep in mind that your message has to be relevant to the topic being discussed. Suddenly exclaiming that you want to ensure that your team has all the resources they need in order to be successful is great except for the fact that coworker Bob only wanted to know if you wanted cream in your coffee.

While you want to state your PR message with frequency, you do not want to put your coworkers to sleep with your broken record. State each item of your PR message in one concise sentence. Rotate your PR message depending on the situation. Your goal is to deliver your message at least three times to three people within three months. Do not bombard them with your message, but do it frequently enough to get it across. There is a balance between subtlety and obnoxiousness.

Finally, to *whom* shall you bestow your glorious message? To everyone. Take no prisoners. Just know your audience. If you are having a difficult time with a coworker, it may be important that they understand you better. You may have to state your PR message on a regular basis and at every interaction. If things are going well with a coworker, it may not be as important to repeat your PR message four times a day, but rather intermittently.

Your PR message helps you articulate your strengths, measure progress, and define and realize your professional legacy. It is one of the many pieces to the puzzle that reinforces your professional image. Remember, to successfully ignite your star power requires that you have a strategy to communicate who you are.

Put It All Together

Be your own champion! Now it is time to put ideas into action. As you work this week, remember to stay focused on your star power and make your message clear. You are special, and it's about time the world, or at least your colleagues recognize that. Think about what makes you unique. Get feedback from your manager and coworkers to see if they agree. Act on your knowledge of what makes you unique. Be on projects and tasks that highlight your strengths, and get one step closer to fulfilling your professional legacy.

Following is your calendar for the week. Plug in what you need to do in Week 6 to make sure you ignite your star power. At the end of the week and before you get ready for a well-deserved weekend, take a couple moments to think back on this week. What went well? What did you learn? What do you want to work on or accomplish next week?

Congratulations on completing your sixth week on the job!

Calendar for Week ⑥ Day ① 2 3 4 5

Time	Action	Notes
6:00 A.M.		
7:00 A.M.		
8:00 A.M.		
9:00 A.M.		
10:00 A.M.		
11:00 A.M.		
12:00 P.M.		
1:00 P.M.		
2:00 P.M.		
3:00 P.M.		
4:00 P.M.		
5:00 P.M.		
6:00 P.M.		
7:00 P.M.		

REMINDERS

► Make time on your calendar to start the process of identifying what makes you unique.
► Schedule times to meet with your trusted friend to discuss your thoughts on your strengths.

Calendar for Week ⑥ Day 1 ② 3 4 5

Time	Action	Notes
6:00 A.M.		
7:00 A.M.		
8:00 A.M.		
9:00 A.M.		
10:00 A.M.		
11:00 A.M.		
12:00 P.M.		
1:00 P.M.		
2:00 P.M.		
3:00 P.M.		
4:00 P.M.		
5:00 P.M.		
6:00 P.M.		
7:00 P.M.		

REMINDERS

▶ Meet with your manager to get feedback.

▶ Find casual opportunities to get feedback from coworkers.

▶ Think about your professional legacy.

Calendar for Week ⑥ Day 1 2 ③ 4 5

Time	. Action	Notes
6:00 A.M.		
7:00 A.M.		
8:00 A.M.		
9:00 A.M.		
10:00 A.M.		
11:00 A.M.		
12:00 P.M.		
1:00 P.M.		
2:00 P.M.		
3:00 P.M.		
4:00 P.M.		
5:00 P.M.		
6:00 P.M.		
7:00 P.M.		

REMINDERS

▶ Find three key phrases that capture what you want to be known for.

▶ Evaluate how you can contribute your strengths to your team.

Calendar for Week (6) Day 1 2 3 (4) 5

Time	Action	Notes
6:00 A.M.		
7:00 A.M.		
8:00 A.M.		
9:00 A.M.		
10:00 A.M.		
11:00 A.M.		
12:00 P.M.		
1:00 P.M.		
2:00 P.M.		
3:00 P.M.		
4:00 P.M.		
5:00 P.M.		
6:00 P.M.		
7:00 P.M.		

REMINDERS

▶ Find appropriate opportunities to share your PR message.

▶ Reflect on your time-management skills. What can be improved so that you act consistent with your PR message?

Calendar for Week ⑥ Day 1 2 3 4 ⑤

Time	Action	Notes
6:00 A.M.		
7:00 A.M.		
8:00 A.M.		
9:00 A.M.		
10:00 A.M.		
11:00 A.M.		
12:00 P.M.		
1:00 P.M.		
2:00 P.M.		
3:00 P.M.		
4:00 P.M.		
5:00 P.M.		
6:00 P.M.		
7:00 P.M.		

REMINDERS

▶ Identify who on your team and among your coworkers you need to send your PR message to more often.

▶ Start your task list for next week.

Chapter 7

WEEK 7 Do Lunch

❚❚Things are really speeding up. Some of my project milestones are coming up soon, and I want to make sure that I have gotten input from all the right people. Now that I think about it, in my first few weeks I was meeting two to three new people a week, but since then, I've been so busy with my projects that the pace at which I'm meeting new people has slowed down. I wonder if the people I've already met have important information related to my project or if there are others I need to meet. In any case, I should probably reconnect with the people I've already met to continue to build the relationship. **❚❚**

MONTH 1

MONTH 2

MONTH 3

Throughout your first weeks at your new job you have been making new contacts, building relationships with coworkers, and over the course of time creating a network. Your network is the culmination of relationships and connections that you have available through the people you know.

Your network is critical for helping you work more effectively, gather the right information, accomplish your objectives, and create a comfortable work environment. In this week, review the progress you have made to develop your work relationships and ensure that you are on track to building a strong network.

 Goals

Think about when you met someone for the first time and it turned out that you had a mutual friend. It is often speculated that there are six degrees of separation between you and every other person on the planet. That's right; all that separates you, morning coffee in hand, and the yak herder having his tea somewhere on the Mongol plains are six other people. Moving a bit closer to home, the number of connections between people gets even smaller. Imagine how few coworkers separate you from everyone else in your company.

Week 7 *Sink or Swim* Skills	Overall Objective: Assess the Effectiveness of Your Network
Goals	Check your network.
Time	Modify your networking time so you make the necessary contacts.
Knowledge	Determine if you know the right people with the right information.
Team	Review and reinforce team relationships.
Image	Determine if your image skills are on track to building your network.

Probably not too many! The more people you know, the easier it is to tap someone in your circle for something you need, whether they have the resource or know of someone who does. Building your network will help you get things done much more easily.

Your goal for Week 7 is to ensure that you continue to build your network. Define your current network, identify opportunities for expansion, and create goals for improving your network.

Who Do You Know?

What is a network? A network is a web of direct and indirect relationships. Networks are composed of three levels. Level 1 of your network is made up of your direct relationships with family, friends, and colleagues. These are people with whom you have direct contact. This may include a range of relationships from the people you socialize with on a regular basis to colleagues that you have lunch with once or twice a year. Picture this as your inner circle of contacts and the core of your network.

Level 2 of your network are people who are friends of friends that you know and are people with whom you do not have a direct relationship. For example, you are at a dinner party and one of your friends mentions that they are having dinner with a friend next week who is a Hollywood producer. How exciting you think . . . you know someone who knows someone in Hollywood. It might be time to share that great idea for a script. You've now got a connection to Hollywood! Picture this second level as the middle ring of your network.

Level 3 of your network is composed of people with whom you do not have a relationship at all and only know of through indirect relationships. For instance, it would be the equivalent of knowing that your friend's Hollywood producer friend knows your favorite actress. If you are one of those individuals who love to brag about who you know, you can now say that a friend's friend is friends with Miss Hollywood starlet. Picture this third level as the outer ring of your network.

How do you know your network is sufficient? Do you have access to a broad network of people that possess knowledge, resources, and in turn also know a broad range of people? If you only have two coworkers that you hang out with and have only met five other people in your company of 250, you need to push yourself to meet more people. If your pool of potential folks to network with is limited, develop relationships with people who do have strong networks so that you can piggyback off their network (i.e., rely on Level 2).

While there is no predefined quota for how many people you need to have in your network for it to be effective, it is recommended that you have a network that contains more than one person. Determine for yourself the current strength of your network.

- ▶ Identify how many teammates and coworkers you have met.
- ▶ How many times have you spoken with these people?
- ▶ How many people in and out of work can you call upon for assistance and information?
- ▶ What are their areas of expertise or resources they have to share?
- ▶ Does your current network support the resources and relationships you need?
- ▶ Who else do you need to meet in your company?
- ▶ What would you like your network to help you achieve?

Based on your answers, what would your ideal network look like? As with any goal-setting process, let's define the components of a successful network so that you can build a more concrete plan for achieving it.

1. Define what your successful network looks like. How many people will you know inside and outside of your company? Do you want to have fifty names that you can call upon at any time for a favor? We recommend at a minimum that you aim for a network that has at least ten people from your company and ten people outside of your company (five of whom are in completely different industries and professions). Create a comprehensive network through meeting people outside of your company, industry, and profession.

2. What will you hear from a colleague that confirms that you have a thriving network? When your name comes up in conversations, what do you want people to say about your networking skills? "Ask Dave about that, he knows everyone."

3. What will it feel like when you have a thriving network? Will you feel like you can call upon a friend for a favor? Will it mean that you will feel secure if you know you can ask a colleague for help? A strong network means that you can rely on others even if they are not your best friends. You are not alone in your work world; you have connections!

Unfulfilled Obligations

After you have defined what a stronger network will look like, turn your plans into actions. First, start with the network you currently have. Make sure you are taking the time to properly care for and nurture the relationships. It is easier to strengthen a relationship than build one from scratch. It is also easier to use the people in your immediate network to expand your relationships than trying to connect with people who are total strangers. If you need to refresh and reconnect with your existing network, the place to start is to follow up on any unfulfilled obligations. Sometimes things fall between the cracks during busy times. In the rush of getting your project done two weeks ago, did you forget to send Maria that phone number? Now is the time to patch up any past due obligations and reinforce your relationships.

Next, follow up with people you have worked with or those who have provided assistance to you. You know the "important but not a priority" list. For instance, that thank-you phone call you owe to Billy Joe for his time a couple of weeks ago when he sat down with you for an hour to go over the basics of animal husbandry. Don't let these things linger. Besides, a follow-up "thank-you" will also leave a good impression on others.

If you really want to seal the deal and reinforce your network relationships, think about what you can proactively provide to the people in your network. Didn't you come across a great article last week on the crossbreeding of zebras and Clydesdale horses that is taking the field of animal husbandry by storm? Billy Joe would love to read about that!

Always be on the lookout for things that you can share with the people in your network.

 Time

Based on your review of your current relationships and your goals for a stronger network, adjust your calendar so that you can accommodate more networking time. Building your network is not an extracurricular activity; it is part of your job. It is especially critical as a new employee to seek out and build relationships with others.

First Things First

To revitalize and expand your network may seem like a big deal and potentially a lot of work. It doesn't have to be. Remember, on the surface, larger goals are quickly made bite-size by creating a task list. You realize that it really just comprises calling back two people to make sure they have all the information they need from you for their projects, sending out five e-mails with information you promised, sending out six thank-you e-mails, and sending out five meeting invitations. Most of this can be completed within a half hour, if that!

Once you identify tasks, ensure you have specific action items you can take. If your task is to get input for your project, create action items on your task list that include sending an e-mail to John and Mary to see if they can meet next week. Once an action item gets placed on your task list, it's one less thing you have to worry about. Furthermore, once it's on your task list, it's easier to keep focused when you have a spare minute between projects to send an e-mail or make a call. Pretty soon, your list will quickly shrink.

Let's get tactical; begin to create a network task list of the people in your existing network you need to reconnect with. Identify individuals that you simply haven't connected with in a few weeks. What specifically do you need to provide them with? What resources can you volunteer? Crafting this list won't take long, and it will focus your attention on what specific actions you need to take to recharge your network.

Start using your task list by prioritizing who you need to follow up with, who you need to contact regarding a project or other work-related inquiry, and who you can share resources with. Remember, it is never too late to follow up with people. Make the overdue items a priority on your list. Make a phone call. Send an e-mail. Take out that task list and get going!

Time to Do Lunch

As in Hollywood, it is important to make the time to do lunch. Food is a great way for people to connect. It's also a chance to get out of the office, whether you meet someone in the company cafeteria, the sandwich shop next door, or at a nicer restaurant with a server waiting in the wings. Lunch meetings are also less intense than conference room or office meetings. In a more social setting the dynamic changes; your coworkers become less like corporate drones discussing the finer aspects of your next team meeting agenda and more like normal people.

Adding food to the mix can relax the mood. Plus, you have the ability to look away from the staring eyes of your colleagues and turn your attention for just a moment to contemplate the art of the salad crouton.

Meeting over a meal gives you the opportunity to spend a little bit more time on small talk and getting to know the person, whereas in conference-room meetings, you tend to spend less time with small talk and more time on the agenda items. Doing lunch is a great, winning combination of fulfilling nutritional requirements and building work relationships. Note: At risk of damaging your image and shrinking your network, adhere to the tenants of good manners: proper use of eating tools, chewing with mouth closed to avoid launching food bits from your mouth, and elbows off the table. See the *Tiffany Guide to Table Manners* for further eating etiquette.

Similarly, coffee with a coworker can have the same effect. It's away from your office or cube, food is readily available, and no one is suffering from the moody symptoms of low sugar levels.

The combination of meal and meeting is a great way to maximize your time.

Manage Your Network Time

As you make building and reinforcing your network a priority and start to carve out in your calendar time for rubbing elbows, bear in mind the purpose of your network time: to build relationships through interactions with another person. There are many things you can do such as a quick e-mail or voice mail that take only a few minutes to reinforce and build your network.

Meetings usually take more time. Being new on the job, it is a good idea to volunteer to attend and seek out every meeting that comes your way. Each meeting provides an opportunity to meet people, learn about the company, and learn more about specific projects. As time goes on, you will want to attend fewer meetings and allocate more time to your specific projects. You will get busy as the weeks progress, and your calendar will not be able to sustain a high volume of meetings. There will be little time left to do the work, and you do not want to have to complete your work during quiet times such as staying late, coming in early, or working from home. Be strategic in what meetings you attend.

 Knowledge

An effective network means that you have the ability to pick up the phone or send an e-mail to one of your colleagues and know that an answer to an important question or resource is on its way. Some of the questions in the Goals section of this chapter asked: How many people can you call upon for assistance and information? What are their areas of expertise, or what resources do they have to share? In this Knowledge section, take a closer look at these questions and assess your network from the perspective of what knowledge your current network has and what additional expertise or resources you want to add to your network.

What Do Your Friends Know Anyway?

Think about the different areas of expertise each of the individuals in your network has. Who has what information? For example, in your network, you may find that Mary has strong research skills. She can get you any kind of information you need from the latest government product regulations in France to what your department vice president likes to have for lunch. Bob knows everyone in finance and can get your purchase order processed quickly. Jane knows the bigwigs in academia and is always on top of the latest economic forecasts for your company's industry.

Think about your network. Do you have the Marys, Bobs, and Janes that you need? What other kind of knowledge would be helpful for you? Finally, who do you need to meet to make sure you have the right people with the right information as part of your network? Here are the steps.

1. As you review the previous weeks, what information or knowledge is required to do your job? What information do you have, and what kind of information requires you to tap into your network? What kind of information might you need down the road?
2. Who do you know, and what do they actually know? Review your network of colleagues. Have they been helpful to you when you needed something? Are they the people with the right information?
3. Who else do you need to meet that has additional information, knowledge, or access that would be helpful? Who do your colleagues know that you will benefit from being introduced to?

This assessment is an important exercise. It gives you a realistic picture of what you can expect from your current network and helps you consider in which direction to expand your network. Think about it this way; your social friends are in your life for specific reasons. You hang out with them on weekends and spend your time in meaningful and meaningless conversation. It's fun, and it serves a social purpose.

Building your network at work is much more intentional. You are there to make a living and create a career for yourself, and so are they. Your network is there to serve a functional purpose. If it happens to be personal as well as professional because you have lots of things in common with your coworkers, then that's a bonus. Don't feel shy about assessing who you know and who else it would be helpful to get to know. It doesn't mean you dump your old coworkers for new ones because they are no longer serving a purpose. It means you maintain your network of existing coworkers and continue to build new relationships.

The Dreaded Introduction

Now that you have determined that it would be helpful to start meeting more people, who do you want to meet, and how do you go about meeting them? Start a conversation, get an introduction, and perhaps initiate a meeting. If you have a list of people you need to meet . . . great. Send them an e-mail to invite them to a meeting or lunch and indicate, specifically, why you would like to meet them. For example, "Hi Jane, I understand you are on top of the latest in economic forecasts. Would you like to have lunch? I'd like to find out more of your thoughts on the predictions for next year since I'm putting together a proposal for a new project." If you do not have a targeted list, go to your manager and teammates and ask them who else they recommend you meet for your current projects.

Don't forget you're a newbie; take the opportunity to introduce yourself when you wander the hallways between meetings and going to the break room. Introduce yourself and find out more about the other person. Use your image and specifically your communication skills to build rapport. Ask questions to create a relationship and find out more about the person. This will give you clues into what they know. You may even tell them about your project and ask if they know of anyone who would have the information you seek.

 **Team**

Make sure you have a strong working relationship with the people on your team. As you go out and "do lunch" this week, keep in mind that you will need to keep building the camaraderie with your teammates. Your team is a bit like your family. In every family, it is important to keep the lines of communication open. To ensure things with your team are healthy and on track, review your relationship with your teammates, identify what relationships need to take priority and with whom you need to make more of an effort, and reinforce your relationship by taking specific actions. Finally, as part of further building your relationship with teammates, consider where there might be opportunities to coach your team.

Review Your Relationship with Your Team

In Week 6, you received feedback and insight from some of your teammates about your performance. The teammates you requested feedback from were probably those you trust and with whom you have developed a good working relationship. This week take a look at your relationship with all the members of your team.

As you review these relationships, consider the kind of team you are a part of. Does your team have common goals? Are there inter-dependencies in which if one individual drops the ball, the entire team suffers? Understand larger group objectives and dependencies to help you prioritize where to build and reinforce relationships with your teammates.

Although your overall goal is to have strong working relation-ships with your entire team, you will want to identify specific critical people who warrant attention. The degree of interdepen-dencies you have with specific team members will determine how much attention you might need to put toward building stronger relationships.

Once you review the interdependencies and begin to prioritize your team relationships, dip beneath the surface and take a closer look at some of the dynamics of your relationships with the people on your team. Here are some questions to gauge how well you are bonding. As you answer the questions, think about both the entire team and any "special" individuals.

- ▶ Are your teammates courteous and respectful in your interactions?
- ▶ Are they comfortable or perhaps a bit threatened by you and the skills you bring to the team?
- ▶ When you asked them for help and information in earlier weeks, were they willing to help?
- ▶ When you asked them for feedback in Week 6, were they forth-coming and willing to provide their time and insight?
- ▶ When there have been social events during and after work, did your team make the effort to invite you?

Hopefully, you are on course to developing great relationships with the people on your team. However, don't be disappointed if there are a few individuals you do not get along with so well. It is natural that there may be a few folks who rub you the wrong way or that you rub the wrong way. It doesn't mean that you should avoid them. Even crabby, grouchy, and misunderstood Robby down the hall needs a little love. Sometimes all it takes to reduce friction and build a better relationship is a few gentle proverbial pokes with a stick to get a person out of their shell.

Your Plan to Strengthen Your Relationships

Now that you have taken a closer look at the social experiment called your team and how you are relating with the other subjects, you can develop a clear plan on where and how to strengthen those team bonds. Even if your relationships are already good, make sure you continue to maintain them by identifying ways to keep them strong.

If some relationships need a little TLC and are not so great, make a concerted effort to get them to a level in which there is no name-calling, late-night crank calls, and special-delivery e-mail viruses. It will be especially important to smooth the rough spots in your team relationships if you are on a highly interdependent team. Create a plan to strengthen these relationships.

Start your plan with who. Identify who on your team you need to create better relationships with. Start by resolving any lingering and unresolved items. Was there something that happened with crabby Robby that never got settled? Such as the time you forgot about your meeting and never apologized? It's impossible to build strong relationships on the memories of unresolved issues. In order to walk hand in hand off into the sunset, you will need to resolve any lingering concerns.

Now that you have surfaced and addressed any historical issues, focus on the future and how to avoid potential problems. Instead of complaining to the other person about their behavior or continuing to do something annoying to them, get clear on what can be done differently. Determine what specific actions you can take to make the relationship better. What requests do you need to make of your teammates that would create a more productive relationship? What new behaviors are you willing to commit to?

These ideas and plans you are developing to make your relationships stronger are all great and dandy but are of no benefit until you do something about them. Pick an appropriate time and place to have a conversation. Make sure the conversation takes place in an appropriate location. Airing your complaints to your teammate in a public space will only make the relationship worse. Ask them to meet you for lunch or make the time to go over to their cubicle or office and ask if they have a minute to chat since there has been something on your mind that you'd like to talk about. If necessary, find a conference room where you can talk privately.

Start Coaching

A coach is a person who teaches and directs another person or group through encouragement, advice, and asking insightful questions. We typically think of coaching as something that occurs in sports. Moving from the world of sports, coaching is now fast becoming an expected interpersonal skill in many companies.

Employees expect that as part of their personal and professional development they will get coached by their manager. There are times when employees will even coach their own managers as a form of managing up.

In addition, coaching as a practice is now extending beyond managers to teammates and peers coaching one another. What does this mean for you? Whether or not coaching is a recognized skill or practice in your company, you will want to be a coach and have effective coaching skills.

Here are some coaching guidelines.

1. Offer your insight or assistance as opposed to providing unsolicited or uninvited input. Some people will ask you explicitly for your help, while others will not. You do not want to overstep your boundaries with peers. If you identify an opportunity where you can help a peer, first inquire if they would like help. If you are a manager, you need to coach regularly.

2. No matter what your relationship with the individual, always phrase your thoughts in the form of a question. This gives the other person the option to take your advice. In some instances, because you asked a question, they come up with their own answers, which they are more committed to. The difference between giving advice in the form of a statement such as "You should dress in a suit if you want to change your image" or a question such as "What are some things you can do to make your image look more professional?" is very important. The power of effective coaching lies in helping others identify and take ownership for new information or changes they identify.

3. Options for how to phrase your questions:
   a. Make it open-ended: "What are some ways you could get additional expertise for your report?"
   b. Offer your opinion in the form of a question: "Have you considered going to finance to get their help?"

c. If the person asks for your advice, offer your opinion and then ask them for theirs: "You should take the report and run the numbers by someone in finance because they would know better. What do you think?"

Most of the time when you coach, keep your questions either open-ended (example 3a) or offer your opinion in the form of a question (example 3b). If you are the kind of person that has a solution to every problem and you can't help but blurt out your solution, put a question at the end of it to see what the person thinks (example 3c). When you employ questions, you camouflage what you know they should do so that they can own their answer and you sound a little less pushy and more helpful.

It is important that your conversation lead somewhere. Whether it is identification of a new idea, where to find a missing resource, or a shift in someone's attitude, effective coaching leads to results. Whatever the person walks away with, make sure they walk away with something they can hold on to, think about, or, more importantly, do differently.

You should try to get a commitment from the other person to follow up with you or commit to follow up with them. In even the briefest coaching conversation, establish a date or time in which you will reconnect. It's good relationship-building skills to see how things went after your conversation. Following up demonstrates that you care about the person and outcome.

Effective coaching focuses on performance and tangible results, and is usually based on changing behavior. One of the greatest challenges to the view of traditional coaching is time. The pace of the work environment is constant and unyielding. Coaching is often thought of as a formal procedure that requires an in-depth conversation. In actuality, there are opportunities to coach all around you throughout your day. Coaching should not be thought of as a task but as a set of skills that can be applied in many of your interactions. You become a stronger team player when you demonstrate your coaching skills by helping others solve their problems.

 **Image**

Last week you spent time identifying, crafting, and practicing your PR message. This week honing your image skills will involve a bit of review to confirm that your PR message is sharp and on target and that you are meeting the right people with the right reputation. Take a look in the mirror to ensure that your image is reinforcing the relationships you are trying to build.

The Company You Keep

As you network with people, keep in mind that successfully navigating the political aspects of your new job requires that you be aware of the company you keep. As a new person who is in the process of developing and communicating your image, it is important that your relationships reflect the image you wish to portray. Certain people in your company may not have the most illustrious reputation or may have baggage that long precedes your arrival. As much as possible, be aware of how your associations impact how you are perceived. As in any social setting, we are often known for the company we keep.

Make your own judgment based on your direct experience. You don't want to get sucked into a political quagmire of rumors and accusations. Each relationship provides value. Manage your relationships accordingly. Be smart. Although these individuals may not be great for your reputation, it doesn't mean that you completely dissociate from them either. Acquaintances are just as valuable in your network as your immediate friends. You may have to work on a project together down the road, or they may be your boss one day. Keep your bridges clean and free of fire hazards.

Your Amazing PR Message

Is your PR message getting traction, or is it limping along like an overcooked udon noodle? Whether it has the impact you are shooting for or needs a tune-up, the most important thing is that you are getting in the habit of sharing your message or dropping in key words that support your values and desired image when you get the opportunity.

Personal PR mastery takes time, and crafting the perfect message comes from honing your words and practicing how you deliver your message. Don't worry about getting the wording of your message 100 percent correct before you share. Your coworkers don't yet know what you want to be known for. Following are some tips to help you ensure your message is delivered and gets heard.

- ▶ *Check your attitude*—Your message must be supported by your emotions. If your message is one of creating relationships but your attitude comes off a bit aggressive, you might want to chill out and convey a more relaxed demeanor.
- ▶ *Believe in your own message*—People will listen to you when you believe in what you are saying.
- ▶ *Share the message*—Communicating your PR message may be a new experience. Like anything new, it might feel awkward at first. After a few practice runs, your message will roll off your tongue.

Ponder Your Interactions

Your image has been evolving over the last six weeks. Some of your changes may have been substantial; others have been slight modifications and polishing of an already well-oiled machine. You have developed your image based upon your new work environment, professional objectives, and further insight into what you want to project. Think about your interactions over the last six weeks. How have your interactions with teammates and coworkers been? In what way have your interactions changed as your image evolved? An effective image supports your ability to have productive relationships with your coworkers and continuously expand your network.

Here are some questions to start your reflection process.

- Are people accessible and easy to meet with?
- Are meetings a time for social interactions or strictly business?
- Are your coworkers aware of your skills or competencies?
- In meetings, when you say something, are people listening?
- Have you received any feedback regarding your image? If so, are there any changes you should make?

Based upon how you have answered these questions, you may want to adjust your PR message and other elements of your communication style. Some of the changes you will want to make are based on the culture of your organization. For instance, you may want to make some tweaks if you find yourself chatting up your coworkers in meetings, only to realize that they just want to get down to business.

Other changes may be more specific to your communication style. If you are finding that people tend not to listen to you and to interrupt, do you think it might be because you are too verbose?

Are coworkers dying a slow, torturous death on the other end of the conference call and too kind to say anything and simply interrupt? You do not want to have the experience of people rolling their eyes when you open your mouth because they know how horrible the experience is going to be. You know the type, and you don't want to be one of them.

There's This Thing You Do

Whether it is picking your face, rubbing your neck, talking too loudly, habitually yawning, bouncing your leg, or tapping your fingers, each of us has an annoying habit that can be a distraction from our desired PR message. Imagine your peer's loss of attention when you try sharing your message of detail orientation while simultaneously picking an errant cuticle from around your thumbnail. Do I really have potentially distracting habits? Of course you do. We all do. Don't pretend you don't know what they are.

There have been plenty of people around you who have complained over the years about the annoying habits you have, whether they were a parental figure, significant other, friend, or previous coworker. If you cannot come up with anything, take the initiative and have the courage to ask a trusted friend or colleague. As you reflect on your interactions and how you come across to people, pay attention to what you could do differently. Ensure that people want to be around you and want to build relationships with you. Don't let those little things drive folks away.

People come back to experiences that are pleasant. How can you make the experience for others more pleasant when they are interacting with you? How can you use your verbal and nonverbal communication more effectively to build relationships?

Nonverbal and Verbal Signals

Your nonverbal communication includes your appearance, body language, and tone. Make sure you are dressed appropriately for the workplace. You've been on the job six weeks now and have noticed how others present themselves physically. Is your cologne driving people away? Did you forget to shower after your lunchtime workout? You don't want an invisible force field that repels both people and insects.

Make sure your body language is open and inviting to others. Closed body language is evidenced by not standing up to greet people when they come into your office or cube and sitting with your arms crossed and brows furrowed. Open body language is inviting and pleasant for others to be around. You greet people with a warm smile and even a handshake, if appropriate. You sit in meetings leaning into the conversation and have a pleasant look on your face that tells people you are happy and engaged.

Your tone of voice makes a huge impression on others. If you sound annoyed, angry, or sarcastic, it will not be a pleasant experience. They want to have a conversation with you that is lively and engaging. Make sure your tone of voice reflects this.

Finally, when it comes to your verbal communication, say what you mean and mean what you say. There must be consistency between your nonverbal and verbal signals. Use words that reflect a positive mood. Remember, no one wants to be around someone who reacts to the world around them as if the glass is half empty. People are more interested in hearing about how the glass is half full. They want to hear your ideas about solutions, not complaints. Make sure your verbal interactions with people are filled with positive language that highlights how you can help and ideas you have for solutions.

This winning combination of intentional and positive verbal and nonverbal communication will reinforce the image you want to portray. It makes building your network a lot easier when people have pleasant experiences when they interact with you.

Put It All Together

It is time to put words into action. As you work this week, remember to stay focused on your networking skills to build a strong network. Your ability to create connections and "do lunch" is one of the keys to your success. Make this a priority and make time for it.

Following is your calendar for the week. Plug in what you need to do in Week 7 to make sure you do lunch. At the end of the week and before you get ready for a well-deserved weekend, take a couple moments to think back on this week. What went well? What did you learn? What do you want to work on or accomplish next week?

Congratulations on completing your seventh week on the job!

Calendar for Week ⑦ Day ① 2 3 4 5

Time	Action	Notes
6:00 A.M.		
7:00 A.M.		
8:00 A.M.		
9:00 A.M.		
10:00 A.M.		
11:00 A.M.		
12:00 P.M.		
1:00 P.M.		
2:00 P.M.		
3:00 P.M.		
4:00 P.M.		
5:00 P.M.		
6:00 P.M.		
7:00 P.M.		

REMINDERS

▶ Identify coworkers you need to introduce yourself to and/or get to know.

▶ Make time on your calendar this week to have lunch with coworkers.

Calendar for Week (7) Day 1 (2) 3 4 5

Time	Action	Notes
6:00 A.M.		
7:00 A.M.		
8:00 A.M.		
9:00 A.M.		
10:00 A.M.		
11:00 A.M.		
12:00 P.M.		
1:00 P.M.		
2:00 P.M.		
3:00 P.M.		
4:00 P.M.		
5:00 P.M.		
6:00 P.M.		
7:00 P.M.		

REMINDERS

▶ Make sure your verbal and nonverbal message is coming across as you intend.

▶ Get back to the people you have unfulfilled obligations to.

Calendar for Week ⑦ Day 1 2 ③ 4 5

Time	Action	Notes
6:00 A.M.		
7:00 A.M.		
8:00 A.M.		
9:00 A.M.		
10:00 A.M.		
11:00 A.M.		
12:00 P.M.		
1:00 P.M.		
2:00 P.M.		
3:00 P.M.		
4:00 P.M.		
5:00 P.M.		
6:00 P.M.		
7:00 P.M.		

REMINDERS

▶ Review your relationship with your teammates. Who do you need to talk to clear the air?

Calendar for Week (7) Day 1 2 3 (4) 5

Time	Action	Notes
6:00 A.M.		
7:00 A.M.		
8:00 A.M.		
9:00 A.M.		
10:00 A.M.		
11:00 A.M.		
12:00 P.M.		
1:00 P.M.		
2:00 P.M.		
3:00 P.M.		
4:00 P.M.		
5:00 P.M.		
6:00 P.M.		
7:00 P.M.		

REMINDERS

▶ Practice your PR message.

Calendar for Week (7) Day 1 2 3 4 (5)

Time	Action	Notes
6:00 A.M.		
7:00 A.M.		
8:00 A.M.		
9:00 A.M.		
10:00 A.M.		
11:00 A.M.		
12:00 P.M.		
1:00 P.M.		
2:00 P.M.		
3:00 P.M.		
4:00 P.M.		
5:00 P.M.		
6:00 P.M.		
7:00 P.M.		

REMINDERS

▶ Make sure you know which people have the information you need.

▶ Start your task list for next week.

Chapter 8

WEEK 8 Map Your Coordinates

❝ I've been so buried in my projects because they've been challenging and fun. Time continues to move so quickly. I can't believe I've been in this job now for two months. Where did the time go? When I first started the job, I had ambitions and goals about where I wanted to be in this company a couple of years from now. I set my sights on maybe getting promoted within the first year. It seems that the promotion process is very structured. I wonder if my ambitions were realistic given what I've noticed. I have made an effort to really explore my new company. The more I discover, the more I like. As I have learned more, I'm also thinking that there may be other opportunities besides a promotion. **❞**

MONTH 1

MONTH 2

MONTH 3

In the previous weeks you have been hard at work paying attention to the immediate demands of your job and ensuring that you have what you need to be successful. As time continues to race by, remain focused on the present demands of your job. However, in order to ensure you stay on course, you will need to raise your sights and direct your attention to the future.

You are far along in the process of exploring your new work-place, and it's important to stop and map your coordinates to ensure that the course you are on takes you in the right direction. Look toward the horizon and define goals for the next six months. Scan the business environment for potential trends and practice balancing the objectives of today with opportunities of the future.

 **Goals**

Wow! You are finishing up your first two months on the job! Isn't it amazing how time flies? One minute you are finding the restroom, and the next minute you are doing lunch with a highly influential figure in your company. You are on your way to showing the people around you your talents and your ability to deliver results.

Week 8 *Sink or Swim* Skills	Overall Objective: Look to Your Horizon
Goals	Look ahead and identify your six-month goals.
Time	Prioritize your projects in conjunction with your goals.
Knowledge	Identify trends or information that will impact you, your work, and your profession.
Team	Share information with your team to help them look and work toward the future.
Image	Align your image with your future goals.

Over the last eight weeks you have focused your efforts on achieving immediate successes, demonstrating your skills, and building relationships. Now that you have begun to build a foundation, it's time to think about the exciting opportunities in your future. Yes, you have choices! You have a virtual menu of career and work options from which you can choose.

You've played it smart by being keenly aware of your environment and noticing the details of how work gets done and how people communicate, and perhaps you've gotten a glimpse at what the rungs of the company career ladder look like. You've watched the kinds of projects your teammates have taken on, and you are beginning to see future opportunities that might be of interest.

Now that you have been on the job for two months, think about where you want to be six months down the road. To whet your appetite, think about what projects you want to be involved in or initiate, new skills you want to develop, or other interests that you have. Time flies, and you will want to make sure you have a strategy in place to make the most of the coming months.

What Do You Want?

First, clearly define what you want before you plant your foot in the sand and take your first steps toward your future. While this may sound simplistic, you'd be amazed to find that there are many people who do not identify what they want. It's easy to work day after day, changing course as obstacles or opportunities appear, to arrive months and even years down the road at a future that has either provided good fortune or perhaps a destiny that could have gone better. Your future should not be a random series of events but a manifestation of setting a clear direction and achieving what you want. Luckily, you are not one for succumbing to a future of random results.

Based on your observations of your new company, determine what you would like to accomplish six months down the road. Begin by asking yourself the following questions.

- ▶ Are there any emerging trends or events that might influence your industry, company, department, or your profession?
- ▶ On what kind of projects do you want to be working?
- ▶ What new responsibilities would you like to have?
- ▶ What new skills or knowledge would you like to develop?
- ▶ What new relationships would you like to establish?

After you identify your goal, you will need to answer one important question: Why do you want it? Let's say your goal is to be on a high-profile project that helps your marketing function identify a new audience for an existing line of products. What about this potential project motivates you? You ponder the question. Being a part of this project will expose you to company leaders, push you to develop strategic thinking and research skills, and might even provide an opportunity for you to get promoted. What about each of these things motivates you? Clearly understanding why you want something provides you with two very important things: momentum while you work toward your objective and gratification when you reach your goal.

When you know why you want to accomplish your goal, you will stay motivated, and when things get challenging, it's easy to remind yourself why you are working so hard. There are some goals that require long hours and sacrifices to your personal life. You do not want to look back on your accomplishments wondering if the hard work and sacrifice were really worth it. It's awful when you ask people about their accomplishments and motivation for working so hard and the answer is for a promotion, and they really don't know why they wanted to get promoted so badly. Despite the sacrifice, accomplishing the objective didn't quite get them what they wanted. When you know why you want to accomplish a specific goal, the potential sacrifices are part of the process, and the destination is that much more rewarding.

Understanding why you want something may require exploring your underlying motives. A good way to do this is to differentiate your interest from your position. Your position on an issue is what you want on the surface. Your interest is the underlying desire for what is prompting your position. For instance, when someone asks for a promotion, they are expressing their desired position. If you dig deeper and ask what the promotion will do for them, you find out that they either want more responsibility, a bigger job title, or a salary increase. These are the underlying interests that motivate their desire. As you take a look at your six-month goal, ask yourself the question: "If I get _____, what will that do for me? What is my underlying interest?"

Finally, once you are clear on your goal and why you want it, the next obvious step is to define success. How will you know when you get it? If you don't know what your destination looks like, you might cruise right past the checkered flag. Review your six-month goal, and determine what success will look like, sound like, and feel like.

Plan Your Goal

You are making progress! As you set your course, it is now important to get you from where you are now to your future. Defining what you want is not as simple as saying "I want to be a part of a project that will lead to a promotion in six months." You are going to have to be more detailed than that. Now that you have determined your goal, why you want it, and the success criteria, you will need to put a plan in place. Your plan needs to include a timeline, tasks, and milestones. Make your goal more manageable by breaking it down into smaller pieces.

1. Define the milestones for your goal. This allows you to better manage your progress and maintain direction.
2. Document your milestones in your calendar.
3. Use your task list to put down the action item(s) required on a weekly basis to get to your milestones. This ensures that you are staying on track to reaching your goal(s), and each week you can look back on what you have accomplished.

Resources

You have the goal. You are building the plan, and now it's time to determine what resources you need to reach success. The resources you will need to successfully achieve your goal will depend on the goal itself. Carefully think through what you need in advance of launching your goal. Clearly define the resources you need, where and how to get them, and when you will need them. This will ensure that you are prepared for success and that you maintain momentum.

Be realistic, flexible, and a bit creative to ensure that you have the resources you require. The quest for resources might be hampered by limited company budgets, opportunities, or even limited time. You don't want your goal to be stopped at the launch pad. Map out what resources you will need and identify potential resource alternatives. Depending on the type of projects you want to be involved in, you may need to develop new skills, meet new people, and even propose a project budget.

Now that you have identified the resources you need to get to your goal, it's time to go get them. Make sure you have identified which resources are critical and possible alternatives. Be ready to negotiate if necessary. In many companies, whether it is someone's time or actual dollars, resources can be scarce, and you will need to be clear on what you need and why you need it.

Ask questions if you need to better understand protocol for getting resources, particularly money. If you need money to take a training course or for other purposes, you will more than likely need to talk with your manager. In this case, it's important to make sure you tell her why you want to do this and what it will do for you and your team.

 Time

Before you light the fuse and blast off toward your destiny, make sure that you allocate and manage your time in conjunction with your goal(s). Your calendar and task list are key ingredients to ensuring your success. Use your calendar to allocate time to work on your goals and use your task list to identify the specifics of what you need to do on a day-to-day basis. Use these time-management tools to help you reach your goals and make them a reality.

Prioritize, Prioritize, and Prioritize!

Your mighty goal is only as good as your ability to plan and deliver. You don't want to be the person who likes to talk about his or her great new ideas and plans but never shows results. In the day-to-day activities of getting your work done, it will be very easy to be distracted and lose focus on your plans. As always, you will need to prioritize your tasks.

Hopefully, your goal can be achieved as part of your job. It may also be the case that your goal requires additional training or work outside of your daily activities. When do you have time for that? There is so much to do! Keep focused and maintain momentum toward accomplishing your six-month goal by prioritizing your work. When you effectively prioritize your work, you will be amazed at your ability to squeeze out the time you need to get it all done.

Even though your six-month goal is on your radar screen, make sure your current projects are still the top priority. As the new person, your company is watching to see if you are successful in delivering your projects. They are also watching how you balance delivering your current projects with your ability to think further out and share your ideas. Maintaining this duality will require you to prioritize immediate deliverables and demonstrate immediate wins, while managing to keep an eye on the future.

Handle Your Business

Yes, like the little prairie dog peering across the vast expanse of the plains, it is important that you, too, look to the horizon. Although we are asking you to raise your head and look at the future, it is critical that you first take care of the business at hand.

If possible, make your new goal a part of your current work. It will be easier to manage your time, and there will be a smooth transition from one endeavor to the next. If this is not a possibility, it is important that you make your six-month goal a second priority to your current projects. As a second-tier priority, you will need to carve out time in your schedule to work toward your six-month goal.

Don't Forgot the Timeline and Milestones

Now that you have your priorities in mind, begin allocating time in your calendar and identifying specific tasks on your task list. First, create milestones you can accomplishment and track. Each milestone that is reached is an opportunity for celebration. You can point to them and say "I did that!" You are on track, and you have accomplished a part of your goal. That feels really good!

Next, set deadline dates for each of your milestones. Make sure they are realistic given current demands. As you identify your milestones and tasks, consider your work habits. If you have a tendency to wait until the last minute to get things done, give yourself early deadlines and front-load the bulk of the tasks. Put the majority of the tasks in the first few months of your plan. In this way, you will feel more pressure to immediately get going and not procrastinate. If you like predictability and consistency, a more evenly laid-out plan might suit your needs. Over the next six months as you work toward your goals, review and revise your plan as needed.

 Knowledge

Now that you've got this great idea about what you want to achieve or be working on in six months, it's time to do some research to determine what information and knowledge is needed to accomplish the goal. Make sure you have the knowledge in place to get to where you want to go. To ensure that you are on track, you are going to look at two areas: emerging trends and influences and required information and knowledge. You will build on the earlier Goals section that asked you to identify the resources you need by looking more specifically at what knowledge you will need in order to be successful.

What's Hot Today and Tomorrow?

Research the object of your heart's desire before you conjure up great images of the fascinating projects you would like to be working on for the goals you hope to achieve in six months. The last thing you want is to set your sights in one direction, only to find later that your company has decided to move in the opposite direction. Where does that leave you? The goal you've been working toward has disappeared because you didn't do your research and talk to more people about the company's future. While there will always be unexpected or unforeseeable changes, increase your likelihood of success by first doing your research.

If you are initiating a new idea in the company, ensure that your proposal has taken into consideration current technologies and practices and is aligned with your company's needs and direction. Your research should include talking to trusted colleagues and finding out more about the company, department direction, and strategy over the next six months and beyond. You also want to find out if similar projects have been attempted in the past and the lessons learned from those projects. What made them successful or not?

Invest your time in projects or skill development that yields a high rate of return to you, your team, and your company. Your research should include a thorough scan of the broader environment including industry trends and potential influences. An industry trend might include industry growth or company consolidation through acquisitions. Influencing factors might include a groundbreaking product, technology, or consumer preference.

When doing your research, ask people in your network outside of work and specifically colleagues in other companies if they are doing similar projects or observing similar trends or influences. Your network can be extremely useful in this process. Be aware of your environment so that you can align your present and future coordinates with the direction of your company and broader industry. Ensure that the projects or goals you set your sights on are relevant down the road.

Connect the Dots

Part two of your quest for knowledge focuses on identifying the specific knowledge or information required to reach your goal. Review the resources you identified as you went through the goal-setting process to ensure you identified the appropriate knowledge and skills. Identify whether you need any additional knowledge and/or resources.

- ▶ What individuals in your team, company, and industry can you turn to for more information and support?
- ▶ What additional research, from the Internet to periodicals, is required?
- ▶ What kind of training or longer educational program or certification will you require?
- ▶ Are there others who have blazed this trail? There is no need to reinvent the wheel.

Team

This week, research and determine the trends you anticipate in the next six months and beyond. Aside from using this acquired information as part of accomplishing your goals, think about what else you can do with this great information. You can share it with your team of course! Your team is the perfect forum in which to share your new learning, broaden your perspective through gathering your team's insight, and create opportunity for collaboration. However, it's not as simple as backing up your newly filled dump truck of knowledge on your team's front door. For maximum benefit, ensure that your valuable information is delivered effectively. Determine what is relevant to share, when to share, and how you will share it.

Why Share?

You want to share your discoveries for several reasons:

▶ You build camaraderie with your teammates.
▶ You validate your findings with your team.
▶ You add value by telling them something they may not have thought about.
▶ You expand your discoveries by getting their insight.

Maybe I Don't Want to Share

Still not convinced that there is value in sharing with your team? Here are a few compelling reasons that will hopefully nudge you toward that warm sharing feeling.

- ▶ If you don't share, it's hard to convey your message.
- ▶ If you don't share, you may come off as sneaky or antisocial.
- ▶ If you don't share, people may not share with you.
- ▶ If you don't share, you miss an opportunity to demonstrate your talents.

What to Share

Now that you're clear on why you want to share, the next question is: What exactly do you share? Share what you've found! In the process of defining your goals and gathering knowledge, you probably learned some interesting things and developed some new insights. We are not suggesting that you focus on announcing your new plans; this might come off as too ambitious in the eyes of your teammates. Share what might be of value to your team that you discovered in the process of creating your plans. What did you learn in your research of emerging trends? What opportunities exist for your team?

You want your teammates to know you are thinking and looking ahead. You are adding value to the team by introducing new ideas and initiating conversations about the relevant research you completed.

What if someone takes your ideas? This can be a risk, and you will want to consider what you share and the audience whom you are sharing with. However, you are in a new environment, and you will want to give your teammates and coworkers the benefit of the doubt. Being a team player has everything to do with taking the initiative and making the assumption that you can trust the people around you. You've got to start with the right attitude if you expect others to reciprocate.

How to Share

How you share is a completely different issue from what you share. If you go into the next team meeting and gloat about your complex and amazing research on the next generation of rocket fuel to hit the consumer market in three months and you are pitching this to a team of rocket scientists, you may look silly. They likely already know this. But if you say you are really excited about the upcoming generation of rocket-fuel technology, your message is different. It's not about "let me tell you what I know." Rather, the conversation is more about "I think this is exciting in how it will impact our work."

Use an approach that inspires a conversation as opposed to a lecture. In this way, you get the conversation going, and teammates will jump in and add their two cents about how they think it impacts the industry. Your conversation can even open up into a brainstorming session about different ways to prepare for that change. It is always best to assume your team is seasoned and already knows the information. Confirm the trend you notice by asking questions about your team's thoughts on the impact instead of lecturing them on something they probably already know.

Now What?

Now that you have poured your heart and soul into sharing with your team, what do you (and they) do with the information? There are some different paths which you can end up on.

▶ What you shared may have led into exploring new perspectives and inspiring others on the team to think in different ways. You've broadened their perspectives.

▶ What you shared helped confirm people's beliefs in the direction of their work, perspectives, and direction. They know they are on the right track with their own projects and goals.

▶ What you shared inspired conversation and provided you with new information that has either confirmed your current goals or prompted you to look at some different options.

Whatever the outcome, sharing this information with your team demonstrated that you are interested in making a meaningful contribution. In addition, you were able to either validate the direction of your goals or learn new information that will influence your goals.

Image

Now that you have identified new goals, it's time to take a look in the mirror and review and tweak your image. Just like a striped jacket and plaid shorts don't work together, you will want to be sure that your image is coordinated with your goals. Review and update your image as part of an ongoing process. Just as seasons change, so should your image. You don't want to be the person in the office holding out for the return of polyester bellbottoms, big hair, and gold chains and medallions.

Add More Salt or Pepper

Adjusting your image to support where you want to be is like the culinary arts; you want to play around with your ingredients to make it the best dish possible given what you have to work with. You may need to add a pinch more salt or a dash of pepper. Adjusting your image should be fun, adding a dash of new style, trying a new behavior, or maybe adding some words to your PR message.

If your goal is to work on a high-visibility project in six months, you may find that the people working on those projects tend to be more seasoned and even perhaps a bit older. They may interact with executives on a regular basis and need to project a professional image to the most senior leaders in the company.

So if you are a jeans- and rock-and-roll T-shirt kind of guy, you may want to clean up that image. "But that's what all the engineers wear," you say. That's nice. Is that what all the high-visibility senior project people wear? Can you simply change your shirt from a T-shirt to a collared dress shirt while still keeping the jeans? That's a simple change. You are the same person who is now projecting a professional image. Giving up the rock-and-roll T-shirt is not too much to have to sacrifice, is it?

Adjusting the ingredients of your image might include shifts in the way you communicate or share information. If your goal is to work on a high-visibility project, you want to demonstrate your ability to think at a strategic level, taking into account multiple perspectives and relationships between individuals and organizations. As such, you will need to communicate your awareness of larger company goals and various interdependencies. Use your knowledge about the industry and how it is impacting your company.

Understand your audience to ensure you are addressing their specific interests. No one wants to know the minute details of your work. Give the audience what they need. Your likely audience for a high-visibility project will be senior individuals who want to know your progress and what the results mean for them, not the nifty new way you've figured out how to efficiently write a software code.

Pay attention to your language and words to make sure it is appropriate for your audience. The rule of thumb you use is

WIFM—"what's in it for me?" No one really cares about the WIFM for you. What's the WIFM for your audience? What are they going to get out of your hard work and efforts? What are they going to get for investing their time to hear your update? Make it worth their while. Tailor your message to your audience.

Your Thermostat

You may have to adjust it to fit your six-month goals. For instance, your current PR message may be that you want to be known as accountable for delivering your projects on time, eager to collaborate with others, and a firm but fair individual.

However, if your goal is to increase your skills to make sure you get on a high-visibility project, your PR message should also now include how important it is that you continuously grow your skills to add value to your projects. So you might say: "My projects are going well. Thank you for asking. I'm enjoying them because I can really use the skills I have. I'm really looking forward to continuing to grow my skills in the upcoming months." Your PR message should not be used to advertise what you want.

The intent of your PR message is to communicate your values and what you want to be known for to a broader audience. In the preceding example, communicating your PR message indicates why you would be a valuable asset to a project team. It's different than requesting or whining that you want to be on a project. If you need to articulate your goals, make sure you identify the appropriate time and place for discussing them with the key people who have influence (i.e., to your manager or project leader).

Here is how to properly separate and apply your goals and PR statement. For example, if your goal is to work on a highly visible project in six months, you will want to communicate the values of hard work and accountability. You want others to know through repetition and delivering a consistent message that you value accountability. When you communicate this value, it makes you an attractive candidate for the project because people know what to expect from you. Conversely, only repeating your goal that you want to be a part of the project sounds like you are nagging and fails to provide others with an understanding of what you can contribute. Thus, regularly repeat your PR message to a broad audience and once or twice communicate your goals to select individuals.

Smooth Operator

As you adjust your verbal and nonverbal communication and PR message to be consistent with your six-month goal, make it a smooth transition. You don't want to go from jeans and T-shirt to suddenly wearing slacks and a dress shirt. That's too quick a transition. It will seem really obvious that you are changing your attire, but not apparent why. "What's your intent?" others may ask. Do you want to get ahead? Are you trying to impress the attractive coworker in the next cube? Are you interviewing on your lunch hour?

Make your wardrobe transition smooth. Continue to wear your jeans and start to immediately shift your T-shirt to a collared cotton shirt. In a month or two's time, switch out of your jeans to a pair of black slacks. In another month's time, switch out your collared T-shirt to a cotton dress shirt. There you have it: transformation!

Similarly, when you make changes to your verbal message, start by adding words or phrases to your existing message. Communicate your revised message selectively to let it bake in your audience's mind. Increase the frequency over the course of time. Over the course of a few months, people will perceive that you've got the skills it takes to be on the new project and that you know how to apply what you've learned.

Adjust your image skills to ensure you reach your six-month goals. The investment that you make on a day-to-day basis will greatly pay off down the road.

Put It All Together

Be your own champion! Now it is time to put ideas into action. As you go through your eighth week on the job, remember to focus on where you want to be six months from now. Map your coordinates. Where are you now, and where do you want to be? The work you do today should lead to something intentional down the road. Focus on gathering the best information you can get your hands on to understand current events, upcoming trends, and how they will affect your goals. Then make your goals a reality and work toward them!

Following is your calendar for the week. Plug in what you need to do in Week 8 to make sure you map your coordinates. At the end of the week and before you get ready for a well-deserved weekend, take a couple moments to think back on this week. What went well? What did you learn? What do you want to work on or accomplish next week?

Congratulations on completing your eighth week on the job!

Calendar for Week ⑧ Day ① 2 3 4 5

Time	Action	Notes
6:00 A.M.		
7:00 A.M.		
8:00 A.M.		
9:00 A.M.		
10:00 A.M.		
11:00 A.M.		
12:00 P.M.		
1:00 P.M.		
2:00 P.M.		
3:00 P.M.		
4:00 P.M.		
5:00 P.M.		
6:00 P.M.		
7:00 P.M.		

REMINDERS

▶ Based on your observations of your new company, determine what you want to do six months from now.

▶ Research if this makes sense according to the larger industry.

Calendar for Week ⑧ Day 1 ② 3 4 5

Time	Action	Notes
6:00 A.M.		
7:00 A.M.		
8:00 A.M.		
9:00 A.M.		
10:00 A.M.		
11:00 A.M.		
12:00 P.M.		
1:00 P.M.		
2:00 P.M.		
3:00 P.M.		
4:00 P.M.		
5:00 P.M.		
6:00 P.M.		
7:00 P.M.		

REMINDERS

▶ Make planning for your six-month goal a priority. Prioritize your current project and be sure to set time aside to research your six-month goals.

Calendar for Week (8) Day 1 2 (3) 4 5

Time	Action	Notes
6:00 A.M.		
7:00 A.M.		
8:00 A.M.		
9:00 A.M.		
10:00 A.M.		
11:00 A.M.		
12:00 P.M.		
1:00 P.M.		
2:00 P.M.		
3:00 P.M.		
4:00 P.M.		
5:00 P.M.		
6:00 P.M.		
7:00 P.M.		

REMINDERS

▶ Determine the resources you need to get to your six-month goals.

▶ Identify what success will look like when you get to your goals.

Calendar for Week ⑧ Day 1 2 3 ④ 5

Time	Action	Notes
6:00 A.M.		
7:00 A.M.		
8:00 A.M.		
9:00 A.M.		
10:00 A.M.		
11:00 A.M.		
12:00 P.M.		
1:00 P.M.		
2:00 P.M.		
3:00 P.M.		
4:00 P.M.		
5:00 P.M.		
6:00 P.M.		
7:00 P.M.		

REMINDERS

▶ Align your PR message with your six-month goals.

▶ Share your research findings on industry trends with your team.

Calendar for **Week (8) Day** 1 2 3 4 (5)

Time	Action	Notes
6:00 A.M.		
7:00 A.M.		
8:00 A.M.		
9:00 A.M.		
10:00 A.M.		
11:00 A.M.		
12:00 P.M.		
1:00 P.M.		
2:00 P.M.		
3:00 P.M.		
4:00 P.M.		
5:00 P.M.		
6:00 P.M.		
7:00 P.M.		

REMINDERS

▶ Dress and act the part based on your six-month goal.

▶ Start your task list for next week.

Chapter 9

WEEK 9   Look in Your Rearview Mirror

▟▌Last week was really great. My projects are on track, and I am beginning to think about the work I want to be doing a few months down the road. I am finally feeling like I am developing some good relationships with coworkers. I am pushing myself to give as much as I can and take from my experiences as much as I can. Overall this attitude is paying off.

"I also want to make sure that others are thinking the same. The weekly team meeting went well, even though I missed the first part of it. I came into the meeting fifteen minutes late because my previous meeting ran overtime and was located in a different building. I felt self-conscious walking into the room late. I guess I should have planned better. It makes me wonder what others think of me and if I'm on track. ▟▌

MONTH 1

MONTH 2

MONTH 3

You continue to successfully navigate the currents, keep your head above the waves, and accelerate through the early weeks on the job. You should be proud of what you've accomplished. Before you continue too far, look back on accomplishments and experiences.

Celebrate your successes and prepare for the rapids and waves ahead by identifying what you can do differently.

In this week, your main objective is to review how you are developing and applying your new skills. This week provides a great opportunity to review your progress and ensure that you are headed for success. Identify what is working well and any areas that need more attention. Think of week 9 as a rest stop: a chance to get refueled, make some tweaks, and get ready for the remainder of your adventure.

 Goals

You are well on your way to success, and like any professional, there are always a few more things you can do to improve your game. Now

Week 9 *Sink or Swim* Skills	Overall Objective: Identify How Well You Are Moving into Your New Job
Goals	Check in with yourself.
Time	Determine and adjust your ability to track time and deliverables.
Knowledge	Determine the appropriateness and effectiveness of your knowledge base.
Team	Determine how you are meeting the expectations of your team.
Image	Determine how you are communicating your message and the level of its effectiveness.

that you've passed the two-month mark for your new job and identified what you want to strive for in six months, take a look at where you are now. Is your boat taking in water, or are you riding high? In your ninth week on the job, you are going to take a look around to see how things are going and identify how you can further successfully integrate yourself into your job. What else do you need to do? What else can you do better? Check in with yourself and be honest. How are you really doing? The easiest way to gauge how you are progressing is to look at how well you are accomplishing your objectives.

On Track or Out to Lunch?

When you first started your job, you identified opportunities to develop your skills. You established goals that focused on your development. Revisit these goals that you set when you first embarked on the job. As you spend more time on the job, there may be new skills that you should develop. You may also find that the skills you initially thought would be important are not so critical.

Your life is multidimensional. So are your goals. As you review how you are tracking with the goals you have established, consider how your development goals support or balance your achievement goals. Both your achievement and development goals are equally important. Achievement goals are all about taking care of business and getting results. Your development goals help you reach your achievement goals and serve you in long-term development. All the goals are interrelated.

Achievement goals help set your sights on a specific destination, and development goals ensure that you are prepared. For example, your achievement goal is to become a scientist. Great! What skills will you need to develop in order to become a scientist? The development goals you identify support your achievement goal to become a scientist. Throughout your life you should have a continual stream of new skills and knowledge you want to develop.

This is your chance to make sure you are on track. Often goals are set with a flurry of dedication, focus, and drive, only to run out of steam halfway through to completion. At other times, a specific goal may no longer be relevant because a project or priority has shifted. Make sure that your goals are still aligned with the direction of your team and company.

Once you have confirmed that your goals are still the ones you need to achieve, make sure you are on course toward achieving them. No matter what the circumstances, achieving goals can be a challenge. There are many distractions and competing demands. Your time gets monopolized by other things. Revisit your trajectory by reviewing the following points.

Achievement Goals

- ► I am on course toward achieving my project goals.
- ► I am clear about what resources I need to achieve my project goals.
- ► I have a plan that is regularly updated to help me achieve my project goals.
- ► I reach each of the milestones I've set for my project goals.
- ► I am clear about what success looks like when I achieve my project goals.

Development Goals

- ► I am on course toward reaching my personal or development goals.
- ► I am clear about what resources I need in order to achieve my development goals.
- ► I have a plan that is regularly updated to help me achieve my development goals.

- ▶ I reach each of the milestones I've set for my development goals.
- ▶ I am clear about what success looks like when I achieve my development goals.

 Time

Now that you are almost a company old-timer, you probably are getting a sense of how quickly or slowly things move in your company. The rate in which things happen, when deadlines are identified, and sense of urgency all reflect the pace of your company. As part of ensuring you are on track and keeping pace, let's revisit two critical building blocks of effective time management: routine and planning. Routine . . . Remember? Get up: 10 minutes; get dressed: 20 minutes; and find pulse: 5 minutes.

That's right; your routine provides a starting point to defining how long it takes to get daily activities completed and a predictable daily and weekly structure. Planning—that's right, identifying what steps will take you from cube farm to corner office. Effective time management is extremely important to achieving your goals and demonstrating behaviors that support your image.

That Daily Routine

Predictable, boring, and rigid are words often associated with the term "routine." Instead, we want you to think of your routine in a different way: Opportunity, excitement, and preparation. Your routine provides you with the opportunity to manage your schedule because you know where your schedule can be adjusted and where things must stand. Excitement—at the thought of the unknown because your routine is ready for the unexpected. Preparation—your routine is the Swiss Army knife of the time management realm; you have a foundation in place to take on any planning challenge. Your routines can take multiple forms including your process for getting ready for work, how you set up meetings or prepare for the following day. It's time to review, revise, and reinstate your routine.

Maybe it has been awhile since you've revisited your daily routines. Have you been relying on luck, whims of the traffic gods, and inflatable-doll passengers to use the carpool lane just to get to work on time? Is arriving on time to meetings a challenge when they are scheduled back to back? Maybe the routines you established a few weeks back are slipping a bit? Take a look at the following points to help you review and revise your routines to ensure that they still fit your needs.

- ▶ Do you arrive early or on time? When do you want to arrive? What would be most helpful for you given how much you need to accomplish during the day?
- ▶ Do you get all of your goals accomplished each day? Do you set realistic expectations, or do you try to squeeze too many things into a day and set yourself up for disappointment?
- ▶ Do you make it to meetings on time? If your company has an unstated policy that meetings start five minutes after the hour, are you arriving at that time, early, or late? If you are arriving early, do you use the time to think about your goals for the meeting? If so, keep up the good work. If you are arriving late to the meetings, what needs to change?
- ▶ Do you need to stop your previous meeting and excuse yourself? Do you simply need to give yourself enough time to get from one company building to the next?

► Do you leave work at a reasonable hour? Are you leaving too early relative to your colleagues? Do you have a legitimate excuse such as child care that forces you to leave early, and do you make it up in the evening hours? Are you leaving too late? Does your significant other get upset because you've ruined dinner plans for the third time this week? If so, are you working too hard relative to your colleagues, or are you not working as smart as you could be?

The purpose of having routines is to enable you to have a structure in place that allows you to manage your time effectively and provides a measure of predictability. For example, as part of your routine for scheduling back-to-back meetings, you always schedule them so that each meeting ends five minutes before the hour. This allows you to get to the next meeting on time. Your routines should be revised to suit your needs and reflect what is customary or standard behavior in your company.

Planning and Delivery

By now you have probably realized that successful, on-time delivery of your projects takes more than luck—it takes planning. Planning is critical unless you are an adrenaline junky that thrives on the rush of the surprise of a suddenly remembered deadline. As you continue your time checkup, review your projects and how you are delivering on them. First, review your project deadlines in your calendar. If you haven't put your deadlines in your calendar, now is the chance to get up-to-date. If your deadlines are up-to-date, good job! Your calendar is the most valuable time-management resource you have. Now that you have updated your deadlines, you will have a better sense of whether you are on or off track.

Once you have dusted off and updated your calendar, take a look at how well you are creating a timeline in which to achieve your goals. Good detailed planning is one thing, but if your timeline and milestones are unrealistic, you are setting yourself up for suboptimal achievement. If your timeline is too aggressive, you might be reaching too far too fast.

In the first weeks on the job make sure you are pacing yourself and delivering results. Remember, you are being measured on how you execute. Conversely, you don't want to spread your delivery dates too far apart because it could appear that you are working too slowly. Think through the larger tasks that will take more time and the smaller tasks that you can quickly deliver. Review and revise your existing project timelines so that you are set up for success.

Delivering your work on time is half the equation. The other half of the planning process is ensuring that the quality of your work is as great as it can be. Sloppy work can be avoided by making the time to review and re-review. What is at stake by submitting sloppy work? It is the image of a competent, high-performance new hire. Even a little typo sends a subtle message that you are not paying attention to detail, not a great speller, or have no time to press the spell-checker button.

Are you rushing through your projects so quickly that you do not have time or make time to review the work you have produced? Before you send anything to anybody, whether it is an e-mail or final project report, take your time and review. A good rule of thumb is to review your documents at least twice before pressing the "Send" button. For really important documents, nothing beats an extra set of eyes: Ask a trusted coworker to review your work.

Finally, make sure you have organized your task list to have all the parts of your project included so that you are always 100 percent prepared. Your task list should be in a format that works for you. Everyone's task list will vary. Some people organize their task list according to when things are due and the highest level of priority. Others just throw things on their task list and make sure everything urgent is taken care of by scanning it. If your task list is working well for you, that's great! If it needs to be slightly tweaked to be more organized, then do so. You will reap the benefits of the extra ten minutes it takes right now to organize it.

Part of successfully managing your time is being able to accurately estimate how long it takes to get things done. Whether it is walking down the hall to your coworker's office, drafting a presentation, or scheduling a meeting, concisely allotting the right amount of time to your activities will maximize the space in your calendar. If you are not the best time estimator, you can improve your skills by tracking how long it takes to get various activities done. Before you proceed, make an estimate for how long it will take to accomplish. When you finish, identify how close or off you were. You can also practice your time-estimation skills by checking your watch before, during, and after your activities to track start time, progress, and completion.

 Knowledge

It's a great feeling when a project lands on your desk or when you have a question that you know just where to turn to find the information you need. By now you are well on your way to building relationships and making connections with coworkers and identifying sources of information and ways to efficiently research and gather data. Building upon your prowess as a savvy networker, researcher, and knowledge gatherer, you want to make sure all of the information and resources you have are on track for serving your needs.

When Would You Like This? . . . Yesterday Would Be Fine

Keeping up with the pace of change is potentially a tiresome affair, and yet that's the way it works in the world in which we operate. Take a look at the pace in your company. How fast do things move, and what are people's expectations for how quickly they want information and answers? You are probably working in an environment where the expectation is for fast and even instantaneous results. Different industries may have a different pace and sense of urgency; a technology firm may have a tendency for a faster pace than a bank. However, no matter what your industry, the pace probably feels fast to you. You are still expected to produce the work of three people in half the amount of time.

As you observe and decode the pace in your company, your ability to match this pace is supported through your ability to quickly access information. You can rapidly generate reports because you know where the information is to be found. You set yourself up for success because you demonstrate that you are in sync with the priorities and demands of your company. You know you are becoming a corporate superhero when you are able to quickly put together a presentation to the top executives in your company. You know where to get the data, and you have the information it takes to quickly produce results. Your confidence level increases when you know you can get the right knowledge and information when you need it.

The average person in a company will not necessarily be consciously aware of the pace of their company or strive to keep ahead with the pace of change. Luckily, you are not the average person. Make sure your pace matches that of the company. Your knowledge resources are essential to keeping up and getting ahead.

In the following sections, you'll review more specific information to ensure your knowledge resources are supercharged and boosting you forward.

Your Gear

As with any game in sports, the quality of your equipment makes a big difference to the success of your game. While you may have fantastic innate talents as a runner, if your running shoes do not fully support your feet, your performance may suffer by a few precious seconds. When you add great equipment, you have an edge on the competition.

As you've been working through the last two months, what new equipment have you picked up to do your job better, and what new equipment do you need to add?

You may have found that you stick to your tried-and-true knowledge resources such as journals, magazines, electronic sites, and conferences. Don't get too comfortable. Are there other knowledge resources yet to be discovered? Make sure you expand your repertoire and look for other resources that can help make a difference in how you do your job. Great golf players start with a good set of golf clubs and balls, and they continue to look for new techniques and equipment to bump up their game. Similarly, your knowledge resources can always use some refreshing.

Opportunities

As you review your progress over the last two months, what opportunities did you actively seek out, and what opportunities dropped in your lap? Hopefully, a combination of both occurred. As you searched for information for your projects, you probably started finding opportunities because you asked probing questions or you were fortunate to be in the right place at the right time. There is a positive correlation between knowledge and opportunity. The more knowledge you have and the more active you are in seeking knowledge, the more opportunities present themselves.

So, you had some great opportunities show up. What did you do with those opportunities? Hopefully, you took advantage of them and didn't shy away. One of the most important things to do when opportunity comes knocking is to explore the possibilities. This could be a great chance for exposure and exciting new learning.

Network

This week is also a great time to revisit your network. How are the lunch meetings and networking going for you? The purpose of your network is to provide you with access to information that would not necessarily be easy to obtain. It's your network of colleagues and relationships that provides you with the insights and information you need to do your job. In review, is your network working for you? Who have you developed relationships with? Have they served you in the way you need? Who do you need to develop additional relationships with to get access to the information you require to do your job?

It's Better to Give

How are you giving back to the people in your network? Building a successful network is dependent upon reciprocity. To reinforce your network, you've got to be able to provide something in return. Remember, your network is not only there to serve you, but you are also there to serve it. The larger your network, the higher the likelihood that you may be called upon by your colleagues for information. You don't need to know everything about everything. However, it is important that your network be aware of your strengths. Ensure that your buddies know what knowledge goodies you can provide.

 Team

Are you meeting the expectations of your team? That's a really tough question. You would hope you are. In this section, take a closer look at whether you are providing the value your team was expecting when they first added you to it. You'll also determine areas for improvement, whether you are the newest team superstar or you need a refresher on emulating team spirit.

Mission (Im)Possible

"This mission, should you accept it, is to . . ." Too late! You've already accepted the mission, and now you're beyond two months into it. It's been fun and a great learning experience. You've played the roles of a detective and superstar. Now it's time to revisit whether you are meeting the expectations of the people who've brought you onto this mission.

What were the expectations that were set when you first came on board? What did your manager and team members expect you would contribute and deliver to the team? Remember all those conversations you had in the first couple of weeks on the job to determine your roles and responsibilities? Are you meeting them? Is your team second-guessing if you were the right choice? Regardless of where they stand, whether they think you are great or not living up to expectations, it's not too late to strengthen your position and become an even stronger, more effective team member.

Go back to your notes of the conversations you had at the beginning of your journey. Determine if you are meeting those early, identified expectations. Ensure that you are on track to meeting earlier expectations and are adjusting to emerging or changed ones. Are you adding value to your team meetings, or are you sitting there like a log? It is extremely important that you contribute to your team not only by virtue of your projects, but also in your interactions with them. Contribute in meetings and attend those social events. "But I'm shy" or "I have nothing to add . . . I'm the newest member of the team," you say. That's not good enough. You've been on the team for two months. You are being looked at as a full-fledged contributing member; so act like one.

The Weakest Link

You want the reputation of being a person who consistently adds value and makes contributions to your team. "But I'm the newest person on the team." That doesn't matter. Remember your star power. You provide some great things to your team. Make sure you offer those skills to the team to help it succeed.

You become the weakest link if you are the person on the team others cannot rely on. Make sure that's not you. It's not just about capability and skills; it's also about follow-through. People know you are doing your best and delivering when you do what you say you will do. Make sure you give your projects the time and attention they deserve. Get back to people when you say you will. Provide regular communications to people who need to know what's happening. Ask for help when you need it and volunteer your assistance when opportunity arises.

 **Image**

As you look in the rearview mirror, your image is a key component to review. How are you perceived by others? If you have done a stellar job at communicating your PR message and displaying the behaviors consistent with your message, then you are well on your way to continued success.

In this section, take a look at how you are perceived, what you have communicated to others, and what could be adjusted moving forward.

Your Overall Message

Let's start with your current PR message. The intent of your PR message is to communicate the important elements of what you want to be known for and to create an association with your message. When someone hears your name, they think of the words and values articulated in your PR message. You are known by what you communicate.

When you walk down the hall, what pops into the minds of your cherished coworkers? Do they see Bob, the know-it-all geek, coming down the hall, or do they see Bob the talented and hard-working team player? While you don't want to run around asking everyone what they think of you, it may be a good idea to ask a trusted teammate or coworker how they think you are perceived by others on the team.

Give It to Me Straight

Your teammates are a great source of feedback. To get to the heart of what you are looking for, you may have to probe and ask lots of questions. People may initially give you an off-the-shelf response such as "Oh, you're doing great." This is good information, but it is not necessarily helpful information. You may want to gently probe further and ask "What do you think the team thinks is great so I can make sure to keep doing it."

It's important to probe gently because you don't want to sound like you are fishing for compliments and are not confident. At the same time, it is helpful to know what you are doing well and identify areas for improvement.

Don't be alarmed if you notice an initial hesitation from coworkers when you ask for their perceptions. They are probably caught off guard. They will likely recover and come back with a response. If their response is slight hesitation followed by a couple of "umms," it may be the case that they are not comfortable telling you that you are not doing so hot. If so, back off the topic and read between the lines.

When you get the feedback about how you are perceived by others and how they think you are doing on the job, you can revisit whether your PR message is working. If your intent is to come across as a hard worker who can be counted on and the feedback you get from your trusted colleague is that others on the team think you are reliable and work hard, then your PR message worked. If it came back as you're doing okay and could probably pick up the pace with your projects, it means that your PR message needs to be stated more frequently or, more importantly, that your behaviors do not reflect your PR message.

If the feedback you request does not come back as chirpy and upbeat as hoped or your trusted colleague hesitates in giving you feedback, read between the lines. You think to yourself, "But I don't know what I could possibly be doing to give people a negative impression." Think hard. Think really hard. Are you sure you don't know what could be causing people to be irritated with you? It couldn't possibly be the same thing that drives your significant other crazy, too, now could it? Maybe you talk too much, maybe you monopolize the conversation, maybe you interrupt people, or maybe you state opinions like they are fact. Watch out for these seemingly minor habits you have. They just might be driving others nuts.

Even if your PR message is up in lights and you are finding that you have a pack of groupies following you around, there is always an opportunity to fine-tune your message. What else can you do to reinforce your message? Your professional image is the first thing people notice and the last thing they remember. Make it work for you!

Your Behavior

As good as your PR message is, it's only as good as the behavior you demonstrate. In order for your PR message to be effective, your words and actions must be aligned. Use the feedback you received to make sure your behavior supports your message. There is nothing more important—from your attire to the way you verbally communicate with others. This is an easy and quick win for you. Here's a quick checklist of items.

- ▶ Am I dressed and groomed in a manner consistent with how I want to be perceived?
- ▶ Do I speak concisely and coherently?
- ▶ Do I take the time to build rapport with others?
- ▶ Do I take the time to ask questions to learn more about the other person's perspective?
- ▶ Do I listen and not interrupt?
- ▶ Do I look at the other person when they are talking (not checking my e-mail, phone, or other electronic equipment)?

Put It All Together

Be your own champion! Now it is time to put ideas into action. As you go through your ninth week on the job, focus on looking in your rearview mirror. Consider where you have been, how are you doing, and where you are going. This is a great time to check in and ensure you are doing fantastically on the job. Two months have passed, and now you are moving into your third month on the job. Make this next month a hit!

Following is your calendar for the week. Plug in what you need to do in Week 9 to make sure you look in your rearview mirror. At the end of the week and before you get ready for a well-deserved weekend, take a couple moments to think back on this week. What went well? What did you learn? What do you want to work on or accomplish next week?

Congratulations on completing your ninth week on the job!

Calendar for Week (9) Day (1) 2 3 4 5

Time	Action	Notes
6:00 A.M.		
7:00 A.M.		
8:00 A.M.		
9:00 A.M.		
10:00 A.M.		
11:00 A.M.		
12:00 P.M.		
1:00 P.M.		
2:00 P.M.		
3:00 P.M.		
4:00 P.M.		
5:00 P.M.		
6:00 P.M.		
7:00 P.M.		

REMINDERS

▶ Make sure you are on track with your goals.

Calendar for Week (9) Day 1 (2) 3 4 5

Time	Action	Notes
6:00 A.M.		
7:00 A.M.		
8:00 A.M.		
9:00 A.M.		
10:00 A.M.		
11:00 A.M.		
12:00 P.M.		
1:00 P.M.		
2:00 P.M.		
3:00 P.M.		
4:00 P.M.		
5:00 P.M.		
6:00 P.M.		
7:00 P.M.		

REMINDERS

▶ How are your time management skills? Do you get to work and meetings on time? Do you leave work on time?

▶ Keep up with the pace of work in your company.

Calendar for Week ⑨ Day 1 2 ③ 4 5

Time	Action	Notes
6:00 A.M.		
7:00 A.M.		
8:00 A.M.		
9:00 A.M.		
10:00 A.M.		
11:00 A.M.		
12:00 P.M.		
1:00 P.M.		
2:00 P.M.		
3:00 P.M.		
4:00 P.M.		
5:00 P.M.		
6:00 P.M.		
7:00 P.M.		

REMINDERS

▶ Meet the expectations your team has for you.

▶ Get feedback about how you are perceived by your colleagues.

Calendar for Week (9) Day 1 2 3 (4) 5

Time	Action	Notes
6:00 A.M.		
7:00 A.M.		
8:00 A.M.		
9:00 A.M.		
10:00 A.M.		
11:00 A.M.		
12:00 P.M.		
1:00 P.M.		
2:00 P.M.		
3:00 P.M.		
4:00 P.M.		
5:00 P.M.		
6:00 P.M.		
7:00 P.M.		

REMINDERS

▶ Update your resources for information.

▶ Do your behaviors support your PR message?

Calendar for Week (9) Day 1 2 3 4 (5)

Time	Action	Notes
6:00 A.M.		
7:00 A.M.		
8:00 A.M.		
9:00 A.M.		
10:00 A.M.		
11:00 A.M.		
12:00 P.M.		
1:00 P.M.		
2:00 P.M.		
3:00 P.M.		
4:00 P.M.		
5:00 P.M.		
6:00 P.M.		
7:00 P.M.		

REMINDERS

▶ Do lunch and make sure your network is strong and growing.

▶ Start your task list for next week.

Chapter 10

WEEK 10 Perform a Reality Check

▟▙ Unlike last week, this week wasn't so great. I went into one of my meetings prepared with new information I gathered about the project. This was information I thought would reinforce the value of this initiative. I was prepared to make my case, only to find that a decision to cut the project had already been made. I had no say in the matter.

"Even more frustrating was that I found out later that this decision had been made even before the meeting, and this was the first time I heard about it. I understand the business reason behind this, but it was still a surprise. I wonder if this is typical for how decisions get made and communicated around here. ▟▙

Last week you spent time looking at where you've been and what you've done, and set the stage for any changes you might need to make moving forward. Now that you have been on the job for over two months, you are getting a better sense of what your company, team, and coworkers are really like. The honeymoon is by all means not over; it is still love. However, you are getting the hang of the quirks and idiosyncrasies that make your workplace unique.

After spending a couple months in a company, you will find that your initial understanding of your company's culture, pace, knowledge-sharing practices, teams, and communication has deepened or even changed completely. The perspective you have now is closer to reality. In this week, you will look at your new workplace through eyes that have more experience and insight than when you started your job. When you define the real work environment, you will be able to anticipate potential obstacles, focus your resources, and make the right choices.

 Goals

During your first weeks on the job, it's tough to figure out a company and how it really operates. You did your research and talked with people, and yet the likelihood that everything is as it seems is

Week 10 *Sink or Swim* Skills	Overall Objective: Identify What the Company Environment Really Looks Like
Goals	Determine the real culture and how to thrive within it.
Time	Determine the speed of the organization, team, and individuals.
Knowledge	Determine how information really gets shared.
Team	Determine how your team really operates.
Image	Determine the image that's valued in your company.

rather remote. The realization and understanding of your company's "uniqueness" usually comes with time and experience. The new perspective you may have regarding your company is part of the integration process. You weren't duped into thinking the company was one way, only to learn that things are a bit different; deciphering the inner workings of a company takes time.

Your goal for your tenth week is to think through how your perspective has changed and what the real work environment looks like. Having this clearer picture of your workplace will help you better prepare or modify your existing strategy for how to succeed. Deciphering your environment will require you to stop and think about how work gets done, how relationships are valued, how politics may play a role, and what defines success.

The Rules

Being new on the job is like starting to play a game with a set of assumptions regarding what you believe are the rules, only to realize after a few rounds that the rules you assumed were in place are different. Surprise! How did that happen? Well, it's their game and their company, and they decided the rules. It's time to get all the rules on the table so you can win the game!

Every company has its own set of rules, processes, and behaviors. These unique elements reflect the culture of your company. Some of these things are visible, easy to point out, and logical in how they support the successes and effectiveness of the company. Other behaviors, processes, and rules that are part of the company culture are less obvious and sometimes invisible, until you stumble upon them in your work. You have probably already inadvertently discovered these little company culture surprises and wondered why they are so. Smart, silly, stupid, or whatever the case, it is important for you to stay open and flexible in your new environment.

Clarifying the "C" Word

"Culture" is a big fancy word, isn't it? Management professor and organization-culture guru Edgar Schein suggests that in order to better define and understand organization culture you should look at it as having three levels.

LEVEL 1—Artifacts: Artifacts are generally visible and readily identifiable. Artifacts in your company might include the structures, work processes, and awards you see on the walls.

LEVEL 2—Values: These are espoused values a company has, such as its goals, strategies, and philosophies.

LEVEL 3—Underlying Assumptions: The basic underlying assumptions a company has such as its beliefs. A company's underlying assumptions are often taken for granted or unconscious.

For example, you walk into a company and marvel at how great it is they have on-site dry-cleaning services. What a convenience for its employees! That's an artifact (level 1). This visible artifact is a physical manifestation of one of the espoused values of the company (level 2) that is "making the work environment comfortable for our employees." The underlying assumption (level 3) is that a comfortable employee is a happy employee and a happy employee is more likely to be productive (because they are not out running personal errands) and less likely to leave.

How does organization culture form and evolve? Organization culture begins with the creation of the company. The founders either intentionally or unintentionally infuse their values into their company. The kernel of a company's culture may blossom from a variety of sources such as an initial set of rules, explicit values that the founders hold, or underlying beliefs.

The manifestations of these values or assumptions then get played out and evolve in the years that follow. Culture becomes a part of the company's DNA. As such, when people come into a company and try to change the culture too abruptly, the system naturally fights back. It treats the new person and his ideas as a virus and attacks it until it dies (i.e., leaves the company) or goes into remission.

When we mentioned earlier that it's important to be careful about pushing against how things get done, it's because organization culture is very hard to change. It takes planning, acceptance, time, and senior-leader support. While you can make a difference in a company and help it be successful, it is unlikely that you will change the company culture.

As you go out and start to look at your company's culture and the ways in which business operates, what are the things you notice on the surface? What values does the company espouse, and what do these really say about the company? Use Schein's model to focus and organize your observations.

> **LEVEL 1**—Artifacts: What are the major artifacts that show up? These are things that can easily be seen. Look at both organizational structure and processes. Are there lots of layers of management, or is it relatively flat with a few leaders? Does your company require tons of paperwork to get even the smallest things done? Does your company provide on-site child care and free drinks? Are operating rules and

procedures visible? For example, some organizations have meeting guidelines posted in every conference room.

LEVEL 2—Values: What do these artifacts say about the company's values? If your company throws a pizza and beer party every Friday afternoon, what does it say about the company's values regarding having fun? Does the company have a mission statement? Does your company clearly state its values? Are the values embedded in how the work gets done? Some organizations make sure their espoused values are visible to every employee by placing values and mission statements on posters, Web site, and ID tags.

LEVEL 3—Underlying Assumptions: What do all the artifacts and espoused values mean about the basic assumptions the company has? What were the things that seemed unique, different, or awkward to you when you first started? These are those things that were obviously different to you, but no one mentioned them because they take them for granted.

How do the artifacts, espoused values, and underlying assumptions display themselves? For example, data point number one: The company checks your bag every time you leave (artifact). Data point number two: The company says it values honesty and integrity (espoused value). Conclusion: Not all employees can be trusted (underlying assumption). As paranoid as this company may be, all three levels of culture are aligned.

Call it a cultural experience. This is your opportunity to play detective. It will be valuable to see the interrelationship or disconnections between your company's artifacts, espoused values, and underlying assumptions. Completely figuring out your new company's culture will take time. However, by simply knowing what to look for, you can very easily start putting the pieces together.

Decoding the culture of your company will help you tremendously to be in sync and thrive.

You Mean This Is What I Got Myself Into?

As you begin to better define your company's culture, don't be surprised to find that your earlier perception of your company may have changed. That's okay. It doesn't mean that you didn't do enough research or that the company deceived you. It's just that initial perceptions are influenced by expectations and a lack of complete information. It's no different than dating someone for the first time and thinking they are everything you want, only to find out two weeks later that you have a greater insight and appreciation of their habits and proclivities. It may still be love; you just have a better and more realistic understanding of why you love them.

How does your current view of your company culture compare to your expectations when you first started? As you make this comparison, keep in mind that when you joined the company you made the best decision given all the information you had. This exercise is meant to have you pay closer attention to your environment. It's not meant to send you into a deep depression about what you've gotten yourself into.

Most company cultures have a combination of things that are great and things that are not so ideal. Just like people, companies are not perfect. Get clear on what you appreciate about your company culture and those areas that may require blinders or a doctor's special attention. The parts that are not so ideal you can keep in an "improvement areas box" in your mind. You don't have to do anything about it; just be aware of it so that you are navigating your workplace with maximum agility.

Your Company's Goal-Setting Process

As part of the goal-setting section, you could probably foresee the question: How does your company set its goals? Company goals are often influenced by desire for greater profitability, expansion or market growth, and creation of new products or services. In turn, your department's goals should be linked to the company's objectives.

Identify whether your department's goals are clearly defined, prioritized, and linked to larger company objectives. If you find that your department is not setting clear goals, it is your job to ask clarifying questions. Ask once. Ask twice, if need be. If you don't get a straight answer, you may have to let it go. Otherwise you'll sound like you are nagging and complaining. If you can't get a clear answer, this typically means that the people at the top are still trying to figure it out themselves. You don't want to make enemies and make them look bad. That would be political suicide. Align your agenda with the company's.

 Time

Last week, you started to take a look at the pace of your company and whether or not your time-management skills were keeping you on top of your game. This week, in order to get a clearer picture and a better sense of your real work environment, you are going to take a closer peek at how time is an influence in your company. The influence of time on your company comes from a variety of sources including your company's industry and the company founders.

Within your company, time may be treated differently based upon department, managers, or type of work. To better decode how time is treated and influences your company, think about it as three layers: company, department/team, and individual. Understanding how time is treated at these levels will help you determine when and how quickly you need to move.

Company Pace

Each company will vary in terms of how quickly things get done. Certain companies may take forever to get a project off the ground, while another company can quickly go from concept to execution. As you look closer at the pace of your company, keep in mind the industry that your company is in, the unique company methods and processes that can either expedite or slow the pace of work, and your company's sense of urgency.

The pace of your company's industry is a powerful influence. Many industries have specific calendars that dictate research and development, production, and market launch. Whether it is the fashion industry that lives by the seasons or the accounting industry that is driven to frenzy each year around April, it's important to understand how the industry influences your company's pace.

Looking within your company, there may be institutionalized methods and processes for how decisions get made and work gets done. These internal mechanisms can greatly influence the pace within your organization. Keep your eyes open for how decisions get made, what steps are involved in introducing a new idea, and how long it takes to get that new idea off the ground.

The pace of your company is also influenced by either a lack of or a heightened sense of urgency. This level of urgency can be simply a part of your organization's culture: "Things are always crazy around here." It can be a response to an external threat such as a new competitor or an internal concern: "If we don't get that new paperweight to market on time, our team numbers for this quarter are squashed." Understanding whether or not your company is chilly-chill or stress-o-rama on the urgency scale, and why, will help you match the pace or even look for ways to tone things down or crank things up as needed.

Determine the pace of your company.

- ▶ Is your company's industry known for being slow or fast compared to other industries?
- ▶ In what ways is your company pace influenced by its industry?
- ▶ What processes either speed things up or slow things down?
- ▶ What is the level of urgency in your group or company and why?
- ▶ What do you need to adjust to keep pace?

Team Pace

Focus your sights away from the broader company to the pace of your department, team, and the teams with which you interact. Don't be surprised if you find wide variations in how time is treated. While the company pace has some impact on the pace of a department or team, the major pacesetter is the department or team leader. How much this individual drives for results and progress determines how fast the department or team moves.

As you take a look at your department and team, determine:

- ▶ What is the pace of my department? How does this compare to other departments?
- ▶ What is the pace of my team? How does this compare to other teams?

- ▶ Is the pace of my department or team on track, too fast, or too slow?
- ▶ What do my department and team need to do to keep up with the pace of others around us?
- ▶ How does leadership influence the pace?

The pace of your department or team will vary from that of the broader company. However, no matter what the pace, the speed should be aligned to support project and goal success. If you find that your team or department is perhaps a bit out of step, there are a few strategic actions you can take. Take a closer look at the specific elements that are perhaps causing things to be out of sync. Your research should be informal and probably stealthy. No point in getting your teammates paranoid that you are looking to root out the causes of organization inefficiency.

If you make some discoveries about inefficient work practices or a pace that needs to be adjusted, think through potential solutions. Share your new ideas to improve how work gets done. Be specific and volunteer to work on any related tasks. If you discover that it is not so much the work process but the workers, just back up slowly and don't make any sudden moves. Unless you are directly impacted by another person's performance, it is probably not worth bringing the issue to the attention of your boss or team at this time.

Individual Pace

When it comes to the individual, there will be an even wider variation among your coworkers regarding how time is valued and each person's pace. You are probably already aware of the diversity of your coworkers' pacing. The extremes are hard to forget. Some folks are super speedy and intense, while others seem to exist in another dimension in which time moves just a little bit slower. Knowing the pace of the people around you will help you know what to expect when you work with them. You will know that Frank requires a bit more time to get things done and Kimmy talks so fast that you will need to take notes to make sure you get the details of her request. Knowing the pace of your coworkers will also help you to make sure that your pace is on track and in sync.

- ▶ How quickly do other people get projects completed?
- ▶ How quickly do others return e-mails and voice mails?
- ▶ What are the hours others work during a typical day?
- ▶ How do you compare? What do you need to do to keep pace with them?

At the individual level, you have the opportunity to influence and change how time is treated. Based upon your insights, you can change your own behavior to better match your environment. You can also demonstrate and model the behavior that you would like others to exhibit.

 ## Knowledge

All right, Sherlock, it's time to do some sleuthing. Information is power. We've mentioned this already, and you know it by experience. It is important to figure out how information gets shared in your company. It's just no fun to be the last person to know. To better understand this, look at the formal and informal ways in which information is shared.

In Broad Daylight

Let's begin our search by looking at what is in the open: the formal ways in which information gets shared. This can include company Web sites, staff meetings, project meetings, and so forth. As you review the public ways in which information is exchanged, there are two key components to keep in mind: What are the channels in which public information is exchanged, and what kind of information gets shared? There are typically a plethora of venues in which formal information gets exchanged. Make sure you identify and access them.

As you review the ways in which information gets exchanged, think about the implications. If there are formal structures in place, what is expected to be shared by you and others in these formal venues? Are people in fact sharing in these venues? What is the purpose of sharing? What is the depth of information that gets relayed? How willing are people to share information? Is information or knowledge held closely or shared easily? These are important questions you need to ask to understand the type and quality of information that's publicly shared.

Behind Closed Doors

Private information sharing is generally where the juicy stuff can be found. No, we are not talking only about gossip. It's about having valuable information so that you can make the best decision possible regarding your work. For example, you hear through a close coworker that your department's budget for next year will be cut. With this information that has not been made public yet, you start to make contingency plans for the project you are about to propose next week.

What people tell you in private and off-the-record can be very insightful. That's why it is so important for you to develop that network. The more people you know, the more likely you will have information. When your network is big enough, someone somewhere will tell you what you need to know.

As you take a look at your company, uncover what information is shared privately versus publicly. You will want to identify whether the messages communicated through informal channels are the same as those presented via formal mechanisms. You will also want to see if news gets out first through informal channels before being communicated through the formal processes. As part of understanding how private communication processes work in your company, keep an eye out for coworkers who seem to have the latest information. Where does this person get it? What kind of relationship do you have with them?

What are the venues for informal information exchange? Break rooms and cafeterias are a great place to garner information. Having lunch out of the office is a great way to get to know people and have conversations that are more expansive than they otherwise would have been on work premises. People seem to let their guard down a little more in these venues.

Then there is the trusted administrative assistant. They are usually privy to tons of great information. While your intent shouldn't be to leach them for information, you may find that a casual "hello, how are you doing" will lead to an interesting factoid here and there. Administrative assistants are valuable friends.

 Team

The great thing about having a team-player philosophy is that you bring to any work setting an attitude and a set of behaviors that enables success. Yes, that team player ethos is a splendid thing! Over the last nine weeks, you have been developing your team-player skills, and you are on the path to becoming the poster child for collaboration. In order to maximize your team-player skills, take a look at how your team and coworkers manifest team spirit. When you have a better sense of how team-player values are put into action, you will know where to focus your team-player skills and energy.

Your School of Fish

Let's start by taking a closer look at your team. If you aren't part of a formal team, then look at a project team in which you are a member. You have had some time to be a part of your team and to get a sense of how well the group works together. At this point, you should be able to assess whether or not your team is indeed a cohesive group of people dedicated to common goals and values group success as much as individual success. On the other hand, your team may be a group of people brought together as part of a function in which there may be little interdependence.

Although the common objectives of your team set the stage for interdependencies, the importance of effectively collaborating and the benefits of strong relationships are universal. Be aware of how close your teammates are and what they value in terms of communication, follow-through, and demonstration of a commitment to each other. In close-knit teams, the team comes first in terms of meeting deadlines and ensuring that team members are each on track to success. Make sure that your behavior and level of team commitment is up to par. Missing a team dinner because you have plans to watch the game might have been all right at your last company but may be a major faux pas with your new team.

C'mon, Trust Me

Here is a sticky subject: trust. Trust is defined by *Webster's* dictionary as "a firm belief or confidence in the honesty, integrity, reliability, or justice of another person or thing."

Do you have a level of confidence in your team or coworkers that if anyone needed help, others would provide it?

Do members interact with one another honestly?

Do they hold back the truth?

What is your level of trust for your team and coworkers? What is the basis for your answer?

Trust is the key to how well a team works together. If members do not feel that they can trust one another, they are less likely to collaborate, communicate effectively, and work to achieve shared objectives. Assess whether your team has trust by observing how the team members communicate with one another, follow through on commitments, and make the effort to assist each other.

Hopefully, you are part of a team in which there is a strong level of trust. If the level of trust is a bit lacking, consider what you can do to increase trust with each of the individuals on the team. Keep in mind that you do not want to get involved in team-related trust issues or attempt to take sides or moderate a solution too early on. Stay neutral (think Switzerland) and make sure that you reinforce your image as a trustworthy individual.

You may not be able to change the team trust, but you can at least ensure that you are in good standing with everyone and are perceived as honest and have a high level of integrity. If there is someone on the team or a coworker that does not trust you or whom you do not trust, it is important to go back and make sure that trust is rebuilt. This will take time and consistently demonstrating a desired behavior.

For instance, if you do not trust another person on your team because you caught them in a lie, take the time to clearly ask for more information or clarification every time you interact with them. After consistently getting the same message over time, you'll find you are on your way to rebuilding trust. If you are the one who has lost someone else's trust because, for example, you were late on a project, consistently communicate your status with them on the next project.

There are ways to rebuild trust if it is broken. It takes willingness, time, and diligence.

 **Image**

So, you think your pinstriped suit looks pretty sharp? This week you want to test some of your assumptions and take a look at whether your company thinks your pinstriped suit makes you look sharp or ready for a Broadway musical. You want to determine the image that's actually valued in the company including the types of image and behaviors that get rewarded and positively recognized.

You Are the Billboard

The visual presentation of your image can be a powerful and effective way to communicate and reinforce your message. You are a walking billboard of your image: What you wear and your body language all advertise who you are. Even if you are having a bad hair day, the show must go on. You are a professional at all times. You have had some time to think about the image you want to create and have begun to support that desired image through your dress and behavior. You have also had time to observe the image and profile of others and how they are perceived.

It's time to review whether or not people are treated differently based on the image they portray and ensure that your image is on track and supports what you want and how you want to be known. For example, does your company seem to reward people who dress professionally more than those who wear shorts and a T-shirt? Do they take certain individuals more seriously because they present themselves in a more conservative manner? What do you need to do to make sure you have the eyes and ears of the right people?

You may find that certain profiles get more attention from senior management than others. This is not a matter of right or wrong, but simply a fact of business life. If you were a senior manager looking at the next generation of organization leaders, you will more likely notice someone who looks the part than someone who presents themselves in a very casual manner. Right or wrong, people will judge you on the image you convey.

Keep in mind that your primary objective is to succeed in your work environment, not to change the company's culture and perception of what a company leader should look like. This latter is an uphill battle and a waste of your time. After you become CEO, you can institute a change in dress policy. Focus your energy on fine-tuning your image to reinforce your success. What about your image could use some adjustment to make sure you get the kind of attention and respect you deserve? If it means putting on a pair of pants and a dress shirt, do that in order to be taken more seriously.

You may also notice that certain kinds of body language get more attention than others. No, we are not referring to sexual body language. It's more about body language that demonstrates enthusiasm for a project versus one that says you are feeling lukewarm and unenthusiastic. You may notice that those who get excited about projects actually get considered for them. Those who show excitement about the outcome of their project, both positive and negative, actually get recognized for the work they did.

What's the body language that gets recognized and rewarded in your company? How do you want to tweak your body language so that you get the recognition you desire?

Look! A Billboard That Talks!

That's right! You not only look good, but you can also make noises! Let's just make sure the noises you make are reinforcing what a superstar you are. Part of tuning your image is understanding the value your company and coworkers place on what gets communicated. You may find that there are some people in your company who are great talkers. While they may or may not produce very much work, they get positive attention from key members of management because they consistently and frequently present information on their work.

You may scratch your head in disbelief that this person is considered a high performer because you are involved in more projects that are even more challenging. What is going on, you may ask. This person is conveying a message that they are involved in a lot of busy complex work. It is not so much that they are doing a lot of work, but the detailed way in which they communicate what they are doing makes the impression that they are very busy with a lot of important things.

Consider how frequently you need to communicate your message and how detailed you might need to be. Sometimes one sentence is not enough to convey all the great work you are really doing.

Beyond frequency and level of message, detail is also the content in other people's messages that gets recognized and rewarded. What words or phrases cause ears to perk up? What spoken values does the company seem to reward? Specifically, what key words or phrases, such as "results" or "customer value," seem to get the attention of others? Understand the key words or phrases that get noticed so that you continue to fine-tune your PR message.

Your keen discernment of the image skills that get rewarded in the company is an important exercise. Developing your image is an evolutionary process. You will need to consistently stay on the lookout for ways to hone and ensure that your image is working for you. Have fun as you develop, change, and adapt your image. Crafting your image is a great way to try a new style, practice your communication skills, and demonstrate to the people around you who you are and the value you contribute.

Put It All Together

Be your own champion! Now it is time to put ideas into action. As you go through your tenth week on the job, it is important to check the reality of your environment. Like any first date, things are not always what they seem. It's better that you live in a realistic world than the one you made up about your company. You may find some of your discoveries surprising and unexpected. You may find a lot of your discoveries have reinforced that you are in the right company and on the right track.

Following is your calendar for the week. Plug in what you need to do in Week 10 to make sure you do a reality check. At the end of the week and before you get ready for a well-deserved weekend, take a couple moments to think back on this week. What went well? What did you learn? What do you want to work on or accomplish next week?

Congratulations on completing your tenth week on the job!

Time	Action	Notes
6:00 A.M.		
7:00 A.M.		
8:00 A.M.		
9:00 A.M.		
10:00 A.M.		
11:00 A.M.		
12:00 P.M.		
1:00 P.M.		
2:00 P.M.		
3:00 P.M.		
4:00 P.M.		
5:00 P.M.		
6:00 P.M.		
7:00 P.M.		

REMINDERS

▶ What are the cultural artifacts, espoused values, and underlying assumptions of your company?

▶ How quickly does your company move?

Calendar for Week (10) Day 1 (2) 3 4 5

Time	Action	Notes
6:00 A.M.		
7:00 A.M.		
8:00 A.M.		
9:00 A.M.		
10:00 A.M.		
11:00 A.M.		
12:00 P.M.		
1:00 P.M.		
2:00 P.M.		
3:00 P.M.		
4:00 P.M.		
5:00 P.M.		
6:00 P.M.		
7:00 P.M.		

REMINDERS

► How quickly does your team move?

► How does information really get shared? How much are you actually privy to?

Calendar for Week (10) Day 1 2 (3) 4 5

Time	Action	Notes
6:00 A.M.		
7:00 A.M.		
8:00 A.M.		
9:00 A.M.		
10:00 A.M.		
11:00 A.M.		
12:00 P.M.		
1:00 P.M.		
2:00 P.M.		
3:00 P.M.		
4:00 P.M.		
5:00 P.M.		
6:00 P.M.		
7:00 P.M.		

REMINDERS

▶ Increase your network to increase information flow.

▶ Create more communication with your team.

Calendar for Week (10) Day 1 2 3 (4) 5

Time	Action	Notes
6:00 A.M.		
7:00 A.M.		
8:00 A.M.		
9:00 A.M.		
10:00 A.M.		
11:00 A.M.		
12:00 P.M.		
1:00 P.M.		
2:00 P.M.		
3:00 P.M.		
4:00 P.M.		
5:00 P.M.		
6:00 P.M.		
7:00 P.M.		

REMINDERS

► Keep pace with your teammates.
► Determine the image that gets rewarded in your company.

Calendar for **Week** (10) **Day** 1 2 3 4 (5)

Time	Action	Notes
6:00 A.M.		
7:00 A.M.		
8:00 A.M.		
9:00 A.M.		
10:00 A.M.		
11:00 A.M.		
12:00 P.M.		
1:00 P.M.		
2:00 P.M.		
3:00 P.M.		
4:00 P.M.		
5:00 P.M.		
6:00 P.M.		
7:00 P.M.		

REMINDERS

▶ Make sure you are clear on your goals and purpose, even if your team and company are not.

▶ Start your task list for next week.

Chapter 11

WEEK 11   Declare Victory

▌▌▌I got some really good feedback from a team-mate regarding some resources I shared with her. Mary said the article I sent her on forecasting was helpful for managing her projects and keeping organized. She also provided me with some useful tips. It feels great that I am building relationships with coworkers.

"In general, I'm feeling really good about my progress. I'm ahead of schedule on my projects, making a strong contribution to the team, and most importantly, I am really feeling like a part of the company.▌▌

MONTH 1

MONTH 2

MONTH 3

It is Week 11, and you are getting close to completing your first twelve weeks. By now, you are becoming a full-fledged member of your team and organization. You have connections, are deep into your projects, and are swimming like a champ. Your hard work deserves recognition!

As part of recognizing your progress, this week you are going to identify highlights of what you have achieved over the previous weeks. You have been through a lot: You swam with the sharks, made new friends, navigated rough waters, and discovered a whole new world.

This week you will continue to apply your skills and move forward on your projects. Focus on identifying how you have improved over the last couple of months and, of course, look at opportunities to polish your skills.

 **Goals**

You spent last week reviewing the realities of your new company and revising your strategies and techniques in response. This week review your goal-setting skills and determine your successes with setting clear goals, milestones, and deadlines. You will also determine areas of improvement to ensure that your goals set you up for your success.

Week 11 *Sink or Swim* Skills	Overall Objective: Determine Your Achievements and Areas for Fine-tuning
Goals	Identify your successes and improvement areas.
Time	Determine your time management skills.
Knowledge	Determine how you can more effectively share knowledge.
Team	Assess your collaboration and coaching skills.
Image	Assess your networking skills and personal PR message.

Formula for Success

This is an exciting time as you are approaching your third month on the job! It's important to review how your projects are coming along and, on a larger level, your technique and methods for goal success. Your success is based on what you achieve as well as learning what it takes to set and accomplish your objectives. Your goals are unique, as well as how you work toward achieving them.

Building your self-awareness for how you reach your goals is important to being able to consistently set and achieve your objectives. Each person's technique is different. Some people need to chart and identify every minute detail; others just need high-level milestones. Some people are procrastinators who need impending deadlines to motivate them, while others like to pace themselves over longer periods of time.

As you identify the goals you have accomplished and are working toward, consider your winning formula. Identify the ingredients in your formula that you want to keep and those that need to be adjusted.

Let's start with comparing where you are today with where you started out. Besides your lucky rabbit's foot, what were the factors that contributed to your success? Was it:

▶ *Good timing?* Were you in the right place at the right time? Did you do enough research (knowledge) to know that certain individuals were important to your project, and when you saw them, did you happen to ask the right questions? Was it really luck of good timing or knowing to ask the right questions?

▶ *Good planning?* Absolutely! You know by now that good planning makes a big difference. Know your milestones and make sure you give yourself enough time for each section of your project.

▶ *Good execution?* Of course! Your ability to plan and then implement your plan is the key. Your ability to quickly and thoroughly plan and actively drive for results is the balance for which every employer is looking. The skills you have and the questions you knew to ask made your ability to deliver a lot easier and more effective.

Delivery for Your Team

There's one final item that is important for you to review before you move on to the next section. As you think about your achievements over the last two-and-one-half months, how did you contribute to the team? This is not about how you were being a team player. This is about whether or not you met the goals and expectations of your team. Did you meet them, exceed their expectations, or fall short?

Your team can be your biggest supporter or your worst nightmare. It has to do with whether or not you met your goals. If they can rely on you to do what you say you will do and deliver a quality product on time, then you increase the likelihood that you are in their good graces. In this section, think about how you are delivering to your team. Do they have to ask you more than once? Do they have to walk you through every step in every piece of the puzzle? Do you actively contribute and support overall team success?

It's important to review your progress and accomplishments to determine what you did that worked and identify what you need to adjust. Think of this as fine-tuning. Like any amazing piece of machinery, whether it is a Steinway grand piano or a twin-turbo Porsche, perform some fine-tuning to maximize your performance.

 Time

Now let's look at the often dreaded subject of time management. The bedrock of every CEO's success is time maximization. As a budding corporate titan, time management needs to be consistently on your mind as a skill worthy of optimization. As you think back over the last two-and-one-half months on the job, review your routine and your ability to prioritize and actually execute your projects in a timely manner.

The Daily Routine

You've gotten into the groove and flow of things at work, and what a great opportunity it is to check in to make sure your time-management skills are helping you deliver. How has your daily routine been working for you? Are you in and out of the office at a decent hour that meets the expectations of both your team and family? As always, make sure you give yourself enough time so that you are not stressed out in traffic and banging your head against the steering wheel for not leaving earlier.

Congratulations if you have your routine down to a science! If you are still fine-tuning your routine, here are some reminders to get you thinking about what you need to do to get your routine working for you. Make sure you arrive at meetings on time. People will not wait for you, nor is it professional to be late.

Return people's calls and e-mails in a timely manner. Yes, you may be bombarded with 200 e-mails a day. You will want to learn to go through them quickly and clear them out at the end of every day so that you start the next day not feeling behind. E-mails are one of those dreaded things that can quickly pile up and leave you feeling like you are behind. Determine if the e-mails are just a FYI (for your information) or a request for you to do something. Those e-mails that are requests end up as action items on your task list, and those e-mails that are FYIs are simply for quick perusing now.

Don't leave it until later unless you desperately need to leave the office. Don't let it pile up! You are too early in the game to let that happen.

The Prioritizing Game

Not everything can be done by tomorrow; you must figure out what needs to be done now and what can wait. What have you been able to successfully prioritize in the last two-and-one-half months? How did it work for you? How have people responded to your ability to prioritize?

If you are the kind of person that has a hard time saying no to people, it's time to get over that. To be the king of prioritization, there are things to which you may have to say no. Most people don't like hearing no; use it sparingly and learn how to effectively say it.

"But I already know how to say no." A simple no can come off as gruff and not collaborative. When you do say no, make sure you provide a reason and offer other options such as a recommendation for when you can provide assistance, other people who might be able to help, or portions that you can do. Help the other person create their own options.

As you take a look at your ability to prioritize, make sure you are prioritizing the right things. It's great that you perform the act of prioritizing. That's the first step. The second step is to make sure what you think is important is also what others (i.e., your manager and team) think is important. Most people start off with the right intent, except that their rationale is not always good judgment. If you are unsure, check with your manager to share those items you consider a priority and why. Get their input to ensure you are on the right track.

Execution Time

Are you executing on schedule? The type of execution we are talking about has to do with getting your work done. Although the word "execution" has a negative connotation, you'll find this word is often used in companies. If you do not execute on the beautiful, elaborate plans you drew up, those plans are worthless. You might as well have done nothing.

Execution is about bringing your plans to life. Think about how you are successfully executing in your work environment. Given what you've learned about the pace of your company, department/ team, and individuals, are you executing in a manner that's consistent with the pace of others? Were you able to deliver on the plans and promises you made?

How have you used various tools and techniques such as your task list to help keep you focused on what you needed to do from one day to the next? Your ability to deliver your high-quality projects in a timely manner is extremely important. Keep up the great work and continue to put your plans into action!

Knowledge

Like the giant net of a commercial fishing ship, you have been scooping up as much information and new knowledge as possible. Some of your catch you have thrown back, and some of what you have gathered is good enough to keep. In this week's Knowledge section, review the information and skills you have acquired and consider ways to make sure you are on track to sharing your knowledge resources with the people around you. You've been a sponge for the last two-and-one-half months, and if you haven't done so already, squeeze yourself and give back.

Skills You Learned

Before you revitalize your strategy for sharing your knowledge, let's take a closer look at the knowledge and information you have gathered so that you are clear on what exactly to share and with whom. Take an inventory of what you have learned over the past weeks and any other bits of knowledge that you think would be valuable to others. As you take inventory, document your knowledge. Consider what you learned and how you found this knowledge. Did you acquire it through the people around you? The classes you took? The literature you read? The research you performed? It's amazing how much information you can acquire in a two-and-one-half month time frame. It is your ability to obtain information that will continue to drive your success. In retrospect, what sources did you find worked best for you? The best way to pick up information is to continue to keep your eyes and ears open and ask good questions.

Who and What You Know

In addition to what you have learned and the skills you've acquired over the last two-and-one-half months, review your network. By now you should have in place a growing network of coworkers and even people outside of your company you can turn to as sources of information. Over the last eleven weeks, we have been poking and prodding you to make sure that you have been not only getting new information and knowledge from the people around you, but also sharing what you know. Before you can declare victory, identify any opportunities to reinforce your network.

Thirty Minutes or Less: Delivery Is Everything

Delivery is not just about pizza. It's also about how you present what you have to share with others. You are just about ready to tighten the bolts on your knowledge network. However, before you grab the phone and start calling your colleagues, let's pause and reflect on your previous forays into the realm of sharing. Consider what has worked well when you have shared and also consider what may not have been so effective. Moving forward, remember to consider these simple rules.

1. *Know your audience:* Identify what specific information is relevant to their needs.

2. *Create a package:* Make the information as usable as possible for your audience. Make sure you put in the WIFM (what's in it for me).

3. *Deliver the package:* Identify the most effective way to share your goodies.

4. *Assess the value:* Follow up with your audience to confirm the value or benefit of what you shared and if there is any additional information that would be helpful.

 **Team**

Your team skills are all about collaboration and coaching. In retrospect, how proactive have you been in building relationships with your coworkers and ensuring that you are making the best effort to be a team player? As you get closer to finishing your first twelve weeks on the job, keep up the momentum and continue to collaborate and coach whenever the opportunity arises. Given your perspective on the real work environment, assess your coaching skills and determine what you need to adjust so as to make sure you continue to move successfully into the work environment.

Lending a Hand

Collaboration skills are the heart of being a team player. In your eleventh week, assess your collaboration skills. From your detective work in the previous week, you've noticed that your work environment may or may not be conducive to a strong team-player atmosphere. This certainly impacts the degree to which you demonstrate your collaboration skills since it may not always be useful or even politically savvy. However, it's always safer to err on the side of being helpful than not.

Determine for yourself where opportunities to collaborate exist and where you may need to proceed with caution. Certain coworkers might always be up for working together whereas others may be standoffish or resent forced teamwork. Don't be discouraged if people didn't initially embrace your willingness to collaborate; just use some savvy and know where and when to make an effort. It may take time for them to warm up and trust you. So just keep plugging away.

Review your collaboration efforts and consider the following questions.

1. Did you step up to the plate every opportunity you got? Did you avoid additional responsibilities for fear of taking on too much?
2. How does your work environment support collaboration?
3. When you did offer your assistance, did you find the experience personally gratifying? Did it strengthen your commitment to your work?
4. How did your collaboration attempts contribute to strengthening your work relationship with the other person?

"Yeah, I am all about collaboration!" You may think so. However, the real test is whether or not others would describe you as collaborative. If perception is reality, what others think about your collaboration skills determines the fine-tuning that may need to occur as you move forward in your job.

To confirm that you are indeed putting the "C" in collaboration, talk to a few coworkers to see if your perception matches theirs. Do you need to jump in and roll up your sleeves to help? Do you need to involve more people in your projects to make sure their needs are reflected in the end product? Do you need to demonstrate that you care about the opinions of others? Your minor tweaks in your collaboration skills will give you a tremendous return on your time and energy invested.

When You Succeed, I Succeed

Coaching skills are a natural extension of your collaboration skills. As you know, coaching is not about your willingness to help others with a few kind words of inspiration. Effective coaching skills are about understanding a challenge or opportunity that someone is facing and working with them to identify and implement a course of action.

Your coaching skills can play a big part in helping others achieve their objectives and help others on your team learn. Each individual on your team comes from a different background and set of experiences. There is a wide array of skills and knowledge. Your coaching skills help your team or coworkers understand and utilize the different perceptions and backgrounds that each person possesses. As you determine how well you've been coaching others on your team, keep in mind that the new insight you provide to your team is the reason they hired you.

How have you been able to coach others on your team? As problems arise, do you help your teammates talk through the situation by asking them questions? This helps them think through the situation. Or do you immediately give your opinion? Do you make the time to hear the situation? What level of fine-tuning do you need to make to your coaching skills to ensure you are successful in helping others?

Regardless of your rank in the company, coaching is about your attitude toward helping others figure out a solution and your skill in asking really good questions that get to the heart of the issue.

 **Image**

You are starting off in your new position by making the right impression with your team, coworkers, boss, and company. Your image skills have been critical to how you are perceived. Your look, attitude, and demeanor have evolved from "this is who I want to be" to "this is who I am." Before concluding that you are a personal PR genius, let's do a quick review to ensure that you are indeed all that you can be. Set your sights on what you've done well with respect to your communication skills, PR message, and network. Then determine areas for fine-tuning to make that professional image stick.

Communication Skills

Your verbal and nonverbal communication skills are the first things people notice when they interact with you. They convey your professional image. You've done a great job in the last two-and-one-half months of making sure you are more intentional than ever about how you portray yourself. A new work environment is always the best place to start fresh and build the impressions you want others to have. Let's determine what you have accomplished with respect to your verbal and nonverbal communication skills.

▶ *Your Professional Look*—What is your look? Do people see you and automatically think you dress the part? How are you making sure you stay groomed and well manicured? Don't let any of this slip. You've done a great job of portraying a professional image.

▶ *Your Body Language*—Do people know when they see you that you are open and willing to help? How are you demonstrating in your body language that you are pleasant and energizing to be around? How are you sitting in meetings (i.e., leaning into a conversation vs. crossed arms and leaning back in your chair)? How are you using your face to convey a positive message (i.e., smiling and making eye contact vs. furrowed brows and looking away at the clouds)?

▶ *Your Active Listening Skills*—How is your ability to listen to others? How are you making sure you let them finish their sentences and not interrupt? Are you repeating key words and paraphrasing what others have said to confirm that you are both listening and understanding their view?

▶ *Your Rapport-Building Skills*—How are you building rapport with others? Are you making small talk and learning about others' professional and personal lives? How are you doing with matching others' voice tone, key words, and body language to be in sync and create comfort and trust?

▶ *Your Request Skills*—How are you making requests of other people? Are your requests specific in terms of what you are requesting and when you need it? Are your requests getting fulfilled? Are you feeling shy or confident about making requests?

As you celebrate your accomplishments in building your communication skills, there are always things you can adjust and can pay more attention to. Developing strong communication skills is a lifetime of work. Keep practicing!

Your Rockin' PR Message

Your PR message helps others create a perception about who you are and what you stand for. You've done a great job of delivering your message with frequency and consistency. Now let's see how it's working for you.

As you walk the hallways of your new company, what PR message have you achieved? As you pass others in the hall, what is the first thought that pops up in their minds about you?

▶ Do they know what you stand for? Did you state your PR message consistently?

▶ Are their perceptions consistent with what you intended in your PR message? Do you behave consistently with your words?

▶ Is the overall PR message working for you? Are people clear about your contribution and values? Is that reflected in the way they treat you as a person and on projects?

As you review what you have achieved thus far in terms of building your reputation, what else would you like to add or subtract from the equation? Would it be useful to fine-tune the content of your message, delivery of your message, or both? Fine-tuning will ensure that you have a pulse on what others perceive and how that is working for you. When there is alignment between how you want to be perceived and how you are perceived, you increase the likelihood that you are considered for certain projects or asked for your ideas and opinions because what you can contribute is clear to others.

Your Connections

You've built an amazing network of contacts throughout the company within such a short time frame. Great job! It's amazing how easy it is to call upon your network to help you get things done. They want to help you. What are your networking accomplishments?

- ▶ Do you know enough people? Did you have someone to call upon when you needed something? Were they willing to help? If they couldn't help, did you ask them to point you to someone they know who could help?
- ▶ Do you know the right people? Who else is not currently in your network of colleagues that would be helpful for you to know?
- ▶ What points have you scored with your network by giving back? Did you make sure you were there for others when they needed you?

Your network has been an investment of time and effort. You extended yourself to others in ways that you had not done in the past. As you continue down the path of success in your new company, your relationships will be there to support you the entire way.

Put It All Together

Now it is time to put words into action so you can be your own champion. As you go through your eleventh week on the job, celebrate your work and achievements. This is your chance to acknowledge your great work and inspire yourself to keep practicing.

Following is your calendar for the week. Plug in what you need to do in Week 11. At the end of the week and before you get ready for a well-deserved weekend, take a couple moments to think back on this week. What went well? What did you learn? What do you want to work on or accomplish next week?

Wow! Week 11 already! Congratulations on completing your eleventh week on the job!

Calendar for **Week** (**11**) **Day** (**1**) 2 3 4 5

Time	Action	Notes
6:00 A.M.		
7:00 A.M.		
8:00 A.M.		
9:00 A.M.		
10:00 A.M.		
11:00 A.M.		
12:00 P.M.		
1:00 P.M.		
2:00 P.M.		
3:00 P.M.		
4:00 P.M.		
5:00 P.M.		
6:00 P.M.		
7:00 P.M.		

REMINDERS

▶ Determine your project achievements and your ability to set clear and achievable goals.

▶ Celebrate your ability to prioritize and implement your plans.

Calendar for **Week** (11) **Day** 1 (2) 3 4 5

Time	Action	Notes
6:00 A.M.		
7:00 A.M.		
8:00 A.M.		
9:00 A.M.		
10:00 A.M.		
11:00 A.M.		
12:00 P.M.		
1:00 P.M.		
2:00 P.M.		
3:00 P.M.		
4:00 P.M.		
5:00 P.M.		
6:00 P.M.		
7:00 P.M.		

REMINDERS

▶ Acknowledge the skills you've learned and how you've been able to use them.

Calendar for Week ⑪ Day 1 2 ③ 4 5

Time	Action	Notes
6:00 A.M.		
7:00 A.M.		
8:00 A.M.		
9:00 A.M.		
10:00 A.M.		
11:00 A.M.		
12:00 P.M		
1:00 P.M		
2:00 P.M		
3:00 P.M		
4:00 P.M		
5:00 P.M		
6:00 P.M		
7:00 P.M		

REMINDERS

► Recognize your ability to get access to the information and people you need.

Calendar for Week (11) Day 1 2 3 (4) 5

Time	Action	Notes
6:00 A.M.		
7:00 A.M.		
8:00 A.M.		
9:00 A.M.		
10:00 A.M.		
11:00 A.M.		
12:00 P.M.		
1:00 P.M.		
2:00 P.M.		
3:00 P.M.		
4:00 P.M.		
5:00 P.M.		
6:00 P.M.		
7:00 P.M.		

REMINDERS

▶ Celebrate your professional image. People respect who you are and what you stand for.

Calendar for **Week** (11) **Day** 1 2 3 4 (5)

Time	Action	Notes
6:00 A.M.		
7:00 A.M.		
8:00 A.M.		
9:00 A.M.		
10:00 A.M.		
11:00 A.M.		
12:00 P.M.		
1:00 P.M.		
2:00 P.M.		
3:00 P.M.		
4:00 P.M.		
5:00 P.M.		
6:00 P.M.		
7:00 P.M.		

REMINDERS

▶ Always be willing to help others.
▶ Start your task list for next week.

Chapter 12

WEEK 12 Raise Your Sails

❚❚ I'm wrapping up three months on the job. I've made it past the company new-hire probation period with flying colors! It's been a great start. It hasn't always been easy. There have been challenges along the way, but I know I made the right decision moving from my former job to this one. I can see being with this company for quite some time. I have made friends and have begun to build relationships with people throughout the company.

"My earlier ambition of getting promoted within one year has expanded. There seem to be lots of opportunities for growth in both my profession and career. The company supports continuous learning and training. With so many choices, I need to think about it and focus on what I want for my future. I guess the most important thing is that I feel like I am a part of this company. It's time to celebrate! **❚❚**

MONTH 1

MONTH 2

MONTH 3

Congratulations! You have reached Week 12. Up to this point, you have laid the foundation for your professional success. You have questioned, planned, documented, assessed, practiced, and learned. You've been busy!

Before you finish this program, you will set your sights on your future. In this week, consider where you are now, what you have learned, and where you want to be one year from now. You will envision your future and set direction. This is a great opportunity to put everything you've learned into practice for the next year. Your *Sink or Swim* skills will only keep getting better with focus, attention, time, and practice.

 **Goals**

You are now a pro at creating effective goals! Like any great athlete, the test of how good you are is to take your skills to the next level. It's time for the big leagues! What's the major league of goal setting?

Week 12 *Sink or Swim* Skills	Overall Objective: Determine Where You See Yourself One Year from Now
Goals	Determine your one-year goal.
Time	Create a plan with specific time frames.
Knowledge	Determine the knowledge and skills you will need.
Team	Determine the collaboration and coaching skills you need to reach your goal.
Image	Determine areas of development for your communication skills, network, and personal PR message.

Create a one-year goal. With the success of a one-year goal, you may even brave the five-year goal. Let's start with the one-year goal for now since you've been with the company for only three months. Put the skills you've learned over the last three months to work. It's time to raise the sails and head toward the sunset.

The Big Picture

What does it mean to think "big picture," and how is it relevant to setting your one-year goal? To sum it up, your life is the "big picture," and a one-year goal is about progress in your life. You have the potential for achieving everything you set your mind on attaining. It will take focus, dedication, and even a bit of hard work. The exciting and wonderful thing is that you have the ability to set a goal and reach it. A very powerful way to think about what you want to achieve is in terms of what you want to create and share with your workplace: your professional legacy.

In every work setting, you have an opportunity to create something that will live on after you leave your team, group, division, or company. Like a fingerprint, the professional legacy you create reflects your unique skills and abilities. Your professional legacy can take many forms including introducing new ways to get work done, a new product or service, or relationships and changes to how teammates and coworkers work together. Your professional legacy is also something that you take with you. It is part of who you are, your professional experience, and your identity.

Your one-year goal is a big deal. You will spend your time and effort driving toward a result. You want that result to be fulfilling for you as a person and also exciting enough that you will keep working toward it despite possible setbacks. To begin identifying your one-year goal, consider the following questions: Where do you see yourself one year from now? What would you find rewarding to accomplish in one year's time? What do you want to be responsible for creating in your job?

Set yourself up for success by considering the realities of your work environment and what you've been able to accomplish in three months. As you think about what you want to achieve, balance the realities of what is possible and at the same time push the boundaries. Don't just make it an easy goal to achieve. It must have meaning to you and push you to bring out the best of your talents.

The Secret Formula

As you are seasoned in setting goals, you know that once you set your sights on something, it's time to go through the stages to make sure you set yourself up for success. As you are still working toward your six-month goal, keep in mind how those two goals might fit together. As with your previous experience of setting goals for either a project or a six-month goal, your one-year goal is no different. It's just bigger and will require a few additional steps and, of course, patience and perseverance.

Make sure your goal is achievable: in your control, clearly defined, and a manageable size that you can accomplish in one year. Write it down. Next, make sure that you have identified any critical resources and dependencies. Determine the milestones that correspond to every stage of your goal. Then identify time frames and dates to each of your milestones. Now you have the winning formula!

Time

As you set your sights on your future and specifically the next twelve months, it will be more important than ever to continue to apply and consistently develop your time-management skills. The last thing you want to happen is to find yourself twelve months down the road, scratching your head and wondering where the last twelve months went with nothing to show. Your time skills are a crucial part of making sure you create realistic timelines and manage your daily calendar and tasks so that you are working toward your goal. You've been doing a great job of this for your projects. Now it's time to apply it to what you want and where you want to be one year from now.

The Details

Now that you've outlined your milestones and attached some dates, the key to managing your time begins with how you allocate your time to various tasks and milestones. Is your timeline too aggressive or not aggressive enough? Did you account for your time and other people's time? What about other interruptions or priorities?

Once you've attached realistic deadlines, create a task list for each of the milestones. In that way, you have a focused list of to-dos at all times, whether your goal requires you to focus more diligently on your current projects or on extra activities you need to do in addition to your regular responsibilities. This is your opportunity to put into practice what you've learned over the last three months!

Knowledge

The wisdom, knowledge, and information from a variety of people around you will play a valuable part in helping you successfully achieve your one-year goal. As part of your fantastic goal, take a closer look at the knowledge resources you will need and when you'll need them. This will help you make sure you have the equipment to set sail into the sunset.

Things You Can Learn

Scientists exploring life in the deepest depths of the ocean have discovered that marine invertebrates will adapt and change behavior based upon their environment. (Wow, a barnacle has coping mechanisms!) As you think about where you want to be a year from now, what does that mean in terms of the skills you need and don't yet have? We know you're just fine the way you are, but just think of the possibilities that open up if you got even savvier in a particular area. What in the world could that area be? What would be most helpful for you to learn this year to get you to where you want to be at the end of that horizon? Given that a sea sponge can improve itself, imagine what you have the power to accomplish!

It Might be Contagious

You have probably realized by now that the most valuable sources of knowledge and information come from the people around you. Whether it's through casual conversations or a more formal mentoring process, the value of what others know will continue to be a critical resource as you progress toward your one-year goal. The people around you hold tremendous amounts of knowledge and wisdom. They are the perfect resource from which to learn. They may provide you with their direct experience and learning, they may point you in another direction, or they may point you to another person who has information on your topic of interest. The key here is people. Create and nurture relationships with others, and you will see a huge window of opportunity open up.

 **Team**

You've heard us repeat over and over again that being a team player is one of your keys to success. Don't forget that; there will still be many opportunities for you to collaborate and coach.

Collaboration

Your collaboration skills are extremely important. You'd be amazed how many people within companies drop the ball when it comes to collaborating. Turf wars, egos the size of a football field, and lack of patience—all of these prevent collaboration from taking place. Yes, the contemporary workplace may not always look like a utopia, and at times, you may feel like an exhausted salmon depleted of fat stores braving the rapids. But do not give up! Continue to lead by example. You've built such a wonderful foundation with your teammates and coworkers, and just like any garden, it takes mainte-nance, a bit of fertilizer, and nutrients.

Don't go it alone. As you take a look at your one-year goal, think about who you want to involve in your effort. Consider trusted coworkers or identified experts would have valuable insight. The earlier you involve others and make them a part of your objectives, the higher the likelihood that they will support you through it because they have a sense of ownership. Given that you're now a pro at collaborating with others, ensure that your one-year goal reflects your willingness to help out and seek help from others.

Coach

While it's important that you continue to help others through coaching, it is also important that you seek coaching in order to get your game to the next level. Coaching will help you figure out what other factors play into your one-year goal that you may not have considered. Just as you don't have all the answers when you coach someone else on your team, your teammates or coworkers don't necessarily have the answers to your questions. They just have to be good at hearing you out and asking good questions to make sure you don't leave any rocks unturned.

 **Image**

As the work world changes around you, so will the need for your image skills to be continually reviewed and modified. Your image will also need to be adjusted as your professional goals change. You have been evolving your image over the weeks to reflect what you want. As you look toward your one-year goal, determine what changes to your image will need to take place. Identify areas of development for your communication, PR, and networking skills. In order to reach your one-year goal, it will be important over the next year to continue to pay diligent attention to how your image is supporting your goal. Remember, you are a professional at all times. Say it, show it, and do it. Don't let it slip, and keep up the good work!

In order for you to be that superstar one year from now, make sure your verbal and nonverbal communication skills are consistent with the professional image that you want.

▶ What will you have to start or continue to do in order to look and act the part of a superstar?

▶ How will you want to talk to people? What's the tone of voice you want to use?

▶ How important are your active listening, rapport-building, and ask/inform skills?

▶ What PR message do you want others to hear?

Message in a Bottle

Your PR message lets others know what is important to you. While you may not run around telling people you can't wait to be considered for the lead on project X, you can certainly tell people that you would find it challenging, rewarding, and a great experience to be able to lead project X. Note the difference in the tone of the two messages. The first one is arrogant and fraught with assumptions. The second is humble, eager, and describes your values. Just like with your six-month goal, it's important to put the emphasis not on what you want, but on the value you bring.

What PR message do you want to send about your one-year goal? How do you want to be viewed by others? As intrigued? As qualified? As excited? You be the judge. This is your goal. Make it your destiny!

Keep Building Your Network

Just because you are at the tail end of the program does not mean you stop paying attention to building and reinforcing your network. Your networking skills are crucial to your continued success. Your relationships will support you when you're up and down. You may think you know enough people, but things change. People leave positions and companies, and they stop returning your phone calls. Don't put all your networking eggs in one basket. Cast your net far and wide!

With respect to your one-year goal, think about who else you need to know. In what direction do you want to grow your network? Is it to meet more administrative assistants? Is it to create more relationships with project managers? Is it to meet other people in different divisions of the company? As you focus on your networking skills and grow your network, make sure that it expands in the same direction as where you want to be. When you surround yourself with like-minded colleagues, you create a network of immense support as you embark on your new journey. Have fun!

Put It All Together

Now it is time to put words into action . . . and not for the last time either! You will continue to do this for the rest of your career.

As you go through your twelfth week on the job, it is important to celebrate all the work and skills you have achieved over the last three months! Congratulations! The attention you paid in the last three months to taking care of yourself and your career has manifested itself into a successful foundation. As you continue through the adventures of life and your career, make sure *Sink or Swim* skills continue to build on the foundation you've already created.

Following is your calendar for the week. Plug in what you need to do in Week 12 to make sure you raise your sails and continue to practice everything you've learned in the last three months. At the end of the week and before you get ready for a well-deserved weekend, take a couple moments to think back on this week and the last three months. You have accomplished quite a bit, and there is much more opportunity on the horizon.

Congratulations on completing your twelfth week on the job! Be your own champion and keep on swimming!

Calendar for **Week (12) Day (1)** 2 3 4 5

Time	Action	Notes
6:00 A.M.		
7:00 A.M.		
8:00 A.M.		
9:00 A.M.		
10:00 A.M.		
11:00 A.M.		
12:00 P.M.		
1:00 P.M.		
2:00 P.M.		
3:00 P.M.		
4:00 P.M.		
5:00 P.M.		
6:00 P.M.		
7:00 P.M.		

REMINDERS

▶ Determine what you want to do and where you want to be in your career one year from now.

▶ What are the milestones and things that must occur for this to happen?

Calendar for Week ⑫ Day 1 ② 3 4 5

Time	Action	Notes
6:00 A.M.		
7:00 A.M.		
8:00 A.M.		
9:00 A.M.		
10:00 A.M.		
11:00 A.M.		
12:00 P.M.		
1:00 P.M.		
2:00 P.M.		
3:00 P.M.		
4:00 P.M.		
5:00 P.M.		
6:00 P.M.		
7:00 P.M.		

REMINDERS

▶ Create a realistic timeline for your goals. Make sure you keep to your timeline and revise as necessary.

Calendar for Week (12) Day 1 2 (3) 4 5

Time	Action	Notes
6:00 A.M.		
7:00 A.M.		
8:00 A.M.		
9:00 A.M.		
10:00 A.M.		
11:00 A.M.		
12:00 P.M.		
1:00 P.M.		
2:00 P.M.		
3:00 P.M.		
4:00 P.M.		
5:00 P.M.		
6:00 P.M.		
7:00 P.M.		

REMINDERS

▶ Determine what you need to learn and know in order to achieve your one-year goal.

Calendar for **Week** (**12**) **Day** 1 2 3 4 (**5**)

Time	Action	Notes
6:00 A.M.		
7:00 A.M.		
8:00 A.M.		
9:00 A.M.		
10:00 A.M.		
11:00 A.M.		
12:00 P.M.		
1:00 P.M.		
2:00 P.M.		
3:00 P.M.		
4:00 P.M.		
5:00 P.M.		
6:00 P.M.		
7:00 P.M.		

REMINDERS

▶ Focus on your image skills. Determine what you want to be known for one year from now and make amazing progress toward it.

▶ Start your task list for next week.

Calendar for Week ⑫ Day 1 2 3 ④ 5

Time	Action	Notes
6:00 A.M.		
7:00 A.M.		
8:00 A.M.		
9:00 A.M.		
10:00 A.M.		
11:00 A.M.		
12:00 P.M.		
1:00 P.M.		
2:00 P.M.		
3:00 P.M.		
4:00 P.M.		
5:00 P.M.		
6:00 P.M.		
7:00 P.M.		

REMINDERS

▶ Collaborate and coach others. Get coaching for yourself from others to help you implement your one-year goal.

CONCLUSION: YOUR INSPIRATION

Now that you have completed this book, it does not mean you stop using your *Sink or Swim* skills. As you continue to practice and hone them, remember to be your own champion.

Your role is to build a strong relationship between yourself and your employer. You have the power to control the choices you make.

1. Always look for opportunities in every situation.
2. Know your strengths and where you contribute value.
3. Know when and how to ask for help.

Best wishes and always remember to be your own champion!

INDEX

About the Authors

Milo Sindell and Thuy Sindell are founders of Hit the Ground Running, a company that provides products and services to strengthen the relationship between companies and their employees, including the *Sink or Swim Online Training Program*. For questions and information, visit *www.HitThe GroundRunning.com*.

Milo T. Sindell, M.S.

Inspired by his first job at fifteen years old working at a cookie store, Milo Sindell has sought to address the question of how to create work environments that tap into the potential of all levels of employees. As a business consultant, Milo has provided a range of guidance to *Fortune* 500 companies including Intel and Sun Microsystems in the areas of strategy development and implementation, change management, organizational design, global-knowledge management-systems implementation, and employee development and integration. Underlying all of his work is the desire to realize the potential of every company's most important asset: their employees.

Thuy H. Sindell, Ph.D.

Inspired by her first job at fifteen years old doing piecework, Thuy has sought to optimize employee productivity and engagement. As a leadership consultant and coach for Mariposa Leadership, Inc., Thuy works with executives and managers to develop their leadership skills in the areas of strategic thinking, influencing, and coaching skills. Her clients have included Charles Schwab, Cisco Systems, Gap, Hewlett-Packard, Ricoh Silicon Valley, Scios, Inc. (a Johnson & Johnson company), Silicon Graphics Inc. (SGI), Sun Microsystems, University of California at Berkeley, Wells Fargo, and Yahoo!.